PERSISTENT YOUNG OFFEN

The Policy Studies Institute (PSI) is Britain's leading independent research organisation undertaking studies of economic, industrial and social policy, and the workings of political institutions.

PSI is a registered charity, run on a non-profit basis, and is not associated with any political party, pressure group or commercial interest.

PSI attaches great importance to covering a wide range of subject areas with its multi-disciplinary approach. The Institute's 40+ researchers are organised in teams which currently cover the following programmes:

Family Finances – Employment – Information Policy – Social Justice and Social Order – Health Studies and Social Care – Education – Industrial Policy and Futures – Arts and the Cultural Industries – Environment and Quality of Life

This publication arises from the Social Justice programme and is one of over 30 publications made available by the Institute each year.

Information about the work of PSI, and a catalogue of available books can be obtained from:

Marketing Department, PSI
100 Park Village East, London NW1 3SR

Persistent Young Offenders

Ann Hagell and Tim Newburn

Policy Studies Institute
London

**The publishing imprint of the independent
POLICY STUDIES INSTITUTE
100 Park Village East, London NW1 3SR
Telephone: 071-387 2171 Fax: 071-388 0914**

ISBN 0 85374 613 3

PSI Research Report 764

A CIP catalogue record of this book is available from the British Library.

1 2 3 4 5 6 7 8 9

PSI publications are available from
BEBC Distribution Ltd
P O Box 1496, Poole, Dorset, BH12 3YD

Books will normally be despatched within 24 hours. Cheques should be made payable
to BEBC Distribution Ltd.

Credit card and telephone/fax orders may be placed on the following freephone
numbers:

FREEPHONE: 0800 262260
FREEFAX: 0800 262266

Booktrade representation (UK & Eire):
Broadcast Books
24 De Montfort Road, London SW16 1LW
Telephone: 081-677 5129

PSI subscriptions are available from PSI's subscription agent
Carfax Publishing Company Ltd
P O Box 25, Abingdon, Oxford OX14 3UE

Laserset by Policy Studies Institute
Printed in Great Britain by Bourne Press Ltd

Contents

Preface and acknowledgements   vii

List of Tables   ix

List of Figures   xi

PART I: BACKGROUND

1. The Young Offender and the Criminal Justice System   3
    Introduction and aims   3
    Juvenile crime   5
    A brief history of juvenile justice   6
    Persistent offending   19

2   Method of Research   25
    Overview   25
    The three sources of information on young reoffenders   28
    The juvenile interview schedule   32
    Discussion of terms   33

3   The Sample of Young Reoffenders   35
    Number of young people arrested three times   35
    Ethnicity   36
    Age   37
    Current education and work circumstances   38
    Sample representativeness   40
    Summary   43

PART II: YOUNG REOFFENDERS AND THE CRIMINAL JUSTICE
SYSTEM

4   Patterns of Arrest   47
    Arrest patterns   47
    Self report of first arrest   49
    Summary   50

5   Patterns of Offending   52
    Number and characteristics of offences   52
    Offending according to the reoffender's characteristics   59
    Offending in company   62

Police action after arrest: the use of bail and custody 64
Offending on bail 65
The value of offences 67
Self-reported offending 67
Summary 70

6   Use of Sanctions 72
The use of cautioning 72
Patterns of disposals 74
Process through the criminal justice system 76
Summary 77

7   Other Aspects of the Reoffenders' Lives 78
Relationship with family and care histories 78
Friendship groups 83
School experiences 84
Current financial support 86
Alcohol and drug use 86
Psychological health and use of services 88
Offenders' views on their own offending 89
General impression during interview 90
Summary 92

PART III: PERSISTENT YOUNG OFFENDERS?

8   The Issue of Persistence 97
Introduction 97
Defining persistent offending 98
Definition One 100
Definition Two 103
Definition Three 106
Case studies of interviewed persistent young offenders 109
Conclusion and summary 119

PART IV: GENERAL THEMES AND OVERALL SUMMARY

9   Summary and Conclusions 127
Young reoffenders 128
Persistent young offenders 130

References 132

Appendices
A.1   Recording form for collecting police information
A.2   List of questions in the interview schedule
A.3   Self-report offences list
A.4   Description of offence types
A.5   Table 8.3 Contact with Social Services

Preface and Acknowledgements

The early 1990s have seen a growing public debate about the possible existence of a relatively small number of young offenders who, because of their *persistent* involvement in criminal activities, account for a large proportion of the offences committed by this age group. Furthermore, concern has been voiced that a number of legislative changes have made it increasingly difficult to deal effectively with these offenders. This debate is not new, but some of the legislative changes are, and there is a conspicuous absence of systematic and representative data relating to young people who offend frequently.

This report summarises the results from a study of persistent juvenile offending commissioned by the Home Office Research and Planning Unit. The study constituted a follow-up study to initial pilot work undertaken by the Home Office on persistent young offenders. Based in two police force areas, this study had three major aims. First, it endeavoured to provide a more reliable estimate of the number of young offenders who offend frequently, and of the numbers and types of offence accounted for by this group of offenders, and to define and identify persistent offending. Second, it examined the functioning of the criminal justice system in relation to these offenders, together with their experiences of criminal justice. Third, it examined the background of these offenders, their criminal histories, families, educational experiences, contact with welfare agencies and drug use.

The central issue in this report is the definition and nature of persistence. Since we seek to understand the implications of different types of 'persistence', a fairly large group of young offenders is included in the study, in order to allow different definitions to be compared. This is not to imply that all the young offenders for whom we present data should be regarded as persistent offenders.

This study was funded by the Home Office Research and Planning Unit and we are grateful to them for that financial support. In addition, we are grateful to the members of our advisory group (Rob Allen, Ben Bowling, John Graham, David Redhouse, David Rigby and Mollie Weatheritt, all of the Home Office, and Chris Sealey of the Department of Health) for their advice and encouragement during this short but intensive piece of research.

We cannot identify many other individuals for reasons of confidentiality, but would like to express our thanks to the social services departments and police forces in the areas that we studied for their extensive help and support. Particular thanks go to Sergeant Andy Gamlen for his tireless and cheerful assistance in collecting the police data. Thanks are also due to the governors of the young offenders institutions (Feltham, Glen Parva, Werrington and Onley) where some of the young people were in custody at the time of interview, and to the managers of the local authority children's homes and secure units who gave us access to interviewees currently being looked after.

We are indebted to the interviewing team – Virginia Bergin, Kevin Dowd, Joe Elliott, Murray Griffin, Ben Hainsworth and Owain Williams – for their efforts in tracking and interviewing the young people. We are also particularly grateful to David Smith, Head of PSI's Social Justice Group and to Alison Wakefield, Lydia Maher and colleagues at PSI for their help in the preparation of this report.

Finally, thanks must go to the interviewees and their families for their time and interest.

List of Tables

Superscript reference numbers in tables refer to the notes at the end of each chapter.

Table 3.1   Number of juveniles aged 10-16 arrested three times or more in 1992, by area

Table 3.2   Sample age distribution

Table 3.3   Current living circumstances

Table 3.4   Representativeness of interviewed sample: interviewees and full sample compared on sex, age, known and alleged offences

Table 3.5   Mean age of interviewed sample on 1 July 1993

Table 4.1   Total number of 1992 arrests for each young reoffender as recorded in their files at police headquarters

Table 4.2   Interviewees' reports of outcome of first arrest

Table 5.1   Outcome of 1992 offences recorded in police files

Table 5.2   Mean offence numbers by area: all alleged and known 1992 offences

Table 5.3   Mean offence numbers by area: known offending only

Table 5.4   Type and numbers of known offences

Table 5.5   Area differences in offence types and numbers

Table 5.6   Total number of offences taken into consideration for each reoffender in the Midlands county in 1992

Table 5.7   Frequency of known offending by sex

Table 5.8   Self-reported offending: ever and last month

Table 6.1   Number of cautions per offender

Table 6.2   Disposals of offences in 1992

Table 6.3   Number of different types of disposal tried with each reoffender in 1992

Table 6.4   Time (days) between offence, arrest and court according to police files and court records

Table 7.1   Reasons for first contact with social services: Midlands reoffenders only

Table 7.2   Interviewees' self-reported drug use

Table 8.1   Number of reoffenders meeting persistence criteria for arrests, known and alleged offending

Table 8.2   Individuals committing 10 or more offences (not including TICs) within each quarter of 1992

List of Figures

Figure 1.1 Use of custody for juveniles during the 1980s

Figure 2.1 Study design

Figure 3.1 Relationship between age and offence rates: male and female reoffenders

Figure 3.2 Current school situation

Figure 3.3 Occupational status of heads of household

Figure 4.1 Interviewees reports of age at first arrest

Figure 5.1 Total number of known offences in 1992 per reoffender

Figure 5.2 Specialisation or diversification of crime: number of types committed

Figure 5.3 Proportions of offenders committing different types of offences at least once

Figure 5.4 Proportion of offences committed with other offenders

Figure 5.5 Proportions of reoffenders committing any offences with others

Figure 5.6 Immediate police action following arrest

Figure 5.7 Bail status of reoffender when offence was committed

Figure 5.8 Proportion of reoffenders committing any offences on bail

Figure 5.9 Value of offences: amount of theft or damage where value is known

Figure 6.1 The main orders and sentences of the Youth Court

Figure 8.1 Definitions of persistence

Figure 8.2 Overlap between different definitions of persistence

Part I

Background

1 The Young Offender and the Criminal Justice System

Introduction and aims

It is not unusual for young people to get into trouble with the police. The majority of those that do so will have only informal or transient contact, but a significant minority will go on to acquire a criminal record at some point in their adolescence. It is well established that approximately a third of male adults will have been convicted of at least one standard list offence[1] by their thirties (Home Office Statistical Department, 1985), and most of these convictions will have been as a result of offences committed when they were juveniles (Farrington, 1986)[2]. However, a much smaller group of young people will *frequently* commit crimes that bring them to the attention of the police, and the research reported here was undertaken to attempt to provide a clearer picture of offending amongst this group of juveniles.

The research arose in response to quite widely held concerns about the possible existence of a relatively small number of young offenders who, because of their *persistent* involvement in criminal activities, account for a large proportion of the offences committed by this age group. Some had also voiced their concern that the criminal justice system was relatively powerless to deal effectively with these offenders.

Much of the debate about the possible existence of this group has been conducted on the level of anecdote and assertion. Consequently, one of the main aims of this study was basic fact-finding: to look at the pattern of juvenile offending in two geographical areas; at the numbers of offences and numbers of offenders; at the backgrounds of the young people committing the offences; and at the operation of the criminal justice system in relation to these young people. More particularly, the second key aim of the project was to identify the numbers of persistent young offenders in these two geographical areas and estimate the proportion of all offences committed by them. From these data it was expected that a more accurate estimate of the number of persistent young offenders nationwide could be made.

These apparently straightforward aims hide a number of more complex issues. First of all, there is no agreed definition of what constitutes a 'persistent' young offender. It was decided at the outset of the study that it would not be helpful to decide on a definition of 'persistence' in advance of the research. By the same token, given that the major focus of the study was on 'persistence', there seemed little point in examining all juvenile offending in the two study areas. Consequently, the sample of young offenders was constructed by taking all those arrested three times or more in 1992 in the two areas. This was felt to be the best way of excluding those juveniles who come to the attention of the police relatively infrequently, whilst maximising the chances of inclusion of those who offend frequently yet are arrested infrequently.

These young people are likely to be atypical of young offenders as a whole. Although three arrests in the course of a year should not necessarily be used as a measure of persistence, this sample can for the most part be considered to represent the 'heavy end' of juvenile offending. Throughout the report the main sample will be referred to as 'young reoffenders'. They should be clearly distinguished from the bulk of young offenders who neither offend nor are arrested as frequently. Although they include most persistent young offenders, reoffenders are a much larger group also including many who are not persistent offenders on any reasonable definition.

The question of how to define 'persistence' has been brought to the fore by the announced intention of the Home Office to introduce a new custodial penalty which will enable the courts to imprison that small number of young people who commit a disproportionately large number of criminal offences. In order to implement such a policy some means of identifying those considered to be 'persistent' needs to be found.

The penultimate chapter in this report considers three possible definitions of 'persistence'. One of these we generated ourselves, and one is taken from previous pilot work undertaken by the Home Office. The third definition consists of the core elements of the criteria that are likely to be used in determining eligibility for the secure training orders targeted on persistent offenders. The number of persistent offenders identified using each of these definitions is considered, and the young people concerned are then compared to the full sample of young reoffenders.

Public discussion of crime, especially where young offenders are concerned, tends to be emotive and characterised by more than its fair share of historical myopia. The first task, therefore, is to set the study in its historical context. The rest of this chapter looks first at some general features of juvenile offending, and then at the development of the former juvenile justice system, now called the youth justice system. The discussion focuses in particular on the tension between punishment and welfare which underlies debates over youth justice. It is the particular resolutions of that tension that have shaped legislation in this area during the last century.

Juvenile crime

One cannot know for certain how much crime is committed by young people. As the British Crime Survey (BCS) shows (inter alia, Mayhew et al, 1989), a high proportion of crime is not reported to the police. In addition, only a minority of those crimes which do figure in the official statistics are cleared up with the result that the age of the offender is known. The best indicator we have of 'youth crime' is the number of young people known to have offended, that is, those who have been cautioned for or convicted of a crime. It has now become almost commonplace to argue that compared with times such as the early nineteenth century, current levels of crime are far from unusual (Pearson, 1975, 1983; Gurr, 1976). However, taking a shorter time-frame – the period since the second world war for instance – there does seem to be some cause for concern. There was, for example, an almost 150 per cent increase in the number of 14-17 year-old male offenders in the population between 1959 and 1977. However, since that time the pattern of recorded juvenile crime has been rather different. In the period from 1980-1990 the number of juveniles cautioned for or convicted of indictable offences fell by 37 per cent, a dramatic turn-around which is discussed in greater detail below.

Nevertheless, it is important to bear in mind that a high proportion of all offences are committed by young people. Indeed, the relationship between age and offending has been the subject of considerable criminological scrutiny. The prevalence of offending peaks in the mid-to-late teens and decreases steadily thereafter (Farrington, 1990). So stable has this relationship been found to be over time and place that it has even been described as invariant (Hirschi and Gottfredson, 1983; Gottfredson and Hirschi, 1990). While such a view has not gone unchallenged (Farrington, 1986) the age-crime curve remains one of the most basic facts of criminology (Smith, 1994). In addition to age, offending is also closely associated with sex. The analysis conducted by the Home Office of the criminal careers of people born in 1953 which found that almost a third of males had been convicted of a standard list offence by the time of their 31st birthday, also showed by contrast that this was the case for only 7 per cent of females (Home Office Statistical Department, 1985). Although numerous, the majority of juvenile crimes are, however, non-violent in character. In 1990, for example, of all indictable offences for which juveniles were cautioned or found guilty, 10 per cent involved violence (Home Affairs Committee, 1993). The majority – 60 per cent – involved theft or handling stolen goods, 17 per cent were burglary offences, and 4 per cent were criminal damage. Finally, offending is for the majority of young people a transient phenomenon. A number of researchers have suggested that most young people commit some offences, which in the main do not lead to significant contact with the police or courts (Belson, 1975; West, 1982), and that the majority of those who are regularly arrested and prosecuted will nevertheless eventually desist. There remains, however, little rigorous data on the reasons that lie behind this desistance.

A brief history of juvenile justice

The last hundred years of juvenile justice have been characterised by dual tendencies best described as 'punishment' and 'welfare'. However, one need look back no further than, say, 150 years, to find a time when children were not only punished with imprisonment, but were also subjected to transportation and even the death penalty. Although there is some dispute about the extent to which adults and children were treated differently by the criminal justice system[3], it seems clear that during the latter half of the nineteenth century, alongside the development of the modern construction of childhood (Aries, 1962; Thane, 1981) came increasing concern about the welfare of children, parallelled by the development of the new professions of paediatrics and child psychiatry, and the emergence of the notion of 'delinquency'.

A variety of social reformers campaigned to protect children from danger and exploitation. One of their key demands was that children should be removed from the 'adult' prison system and placed in privately managed, state-funded institutions. In addition, such institutions would also be a source of succour for the orphaned and the destitute. One of the most vocal social reformers was Mary Carpenter, who argued that three types of institution were required, *free schools* for the deprived, *industrial schools* for young vagrants and beggars, and *reformatories* for convicted youngsters (Rutherford, 1986).

Statutory provision for reformatories began in 1854[4] and industrial schools in 1857, and one commentator has suggested that the 'acceptance of Mary Carpenter's belief that children should not be dealt with as men [sic], but as children, was a seminal point in the evolution of the modern child' (May, 1973). However, one of the unintended consequences of the introduction of the reformatories and industrial schools was the rapid increase in the number of young people in institutions. According to Rutherford (1986), 'by 1858 only four years after the enabling legislation there were 45 reformatories holding 2,000 young people. Twelve years later there were 65 reformatories holding 7,000 young people'. Much of the later history of juvenile justice in England and Wales follows a broadly similar pattern of attempts at reform – often dominated by welfarist concerns – followed by an increase in the size of the incarcerated juvenile population.

Most histories of juvenile justice begin near the turn of the century with the development of the juvenile court (see for example Platt, 1969). In the mid-1890s, Asquith, the Home Secretary, set up two departmental committees to examine the penal system. The first, the Gladstone Committee, examined the prison system, and the second, chaired by Sir Godfrey Lushington, reformatories and industrial schools. The split between 'punishment' and 'welfare' was evident in the products of these two committees, with the Gladstone Report advocating 'treatment' alongside punishment in prisons, particularly in the case of young prisoners, and the Lushington Committee, in contrast, advocating alternatives to imprisonment, looking in particular to education as one of the remedies for juvenile crime.

By the turn of the century a number of towns were operating separate juvenile courts, and the election in 1906 of a reformist Liberal government ensured that they were put on a statutory footing, at approximately the same time as the statutory creation of probation, of preventive detention and provision for 'borstal training'. The Probation of Offenders Act was enacted in 1907, followed by the Children Act 1908 (the 'Children's Charter') and the Prevention of Crime Act of the same year. The Children Act barred under 14s from prison and provided that 14-15 year-olds could go to prison only if the court issued an 'unruly' certificate. It included sections dealing with the prevention of cruelty to children and referred to begging and prostitution, but is best known for establishing juvenile courts. These courts were empowered to act not only in criminal cases but also in cases of begging and vagrancy. They remained, in essence though, criminal courts.

The Prevention of Crime Act of the same year included provision for 'borstal' institutions. These were intended to cater for the type of person (16-21 year-olds – the 'juvenile-adult category') who 'by reason of his criminal habits and tendencies or associations with persons of such character, it is expedient that he should be subject to detention for such a term and such instruction and discipline as appears most conducive to his reformation and the repression of crime' (quoted in Garland, 1985). It was some time, however, before any distinctive borstal regime developed. Borstal training involved a semi-determinate custodial sentence (the date of release was determined by Prison Commissioners) of one to three years and release was followed by a period of supervision for a minimum of six months. The aims of the borstal institutions were defined as 'reformation' and training', and these were achieved through 'physical exercise, moral instruction, [and] industrial or agricultural training' (Garland, 1985).

Interestingly, the same legislation included provision for dealing with 'habitual criminals' through preventive detention. Habitual criminals were those who led 'persistently a dishonest or criminal life' and who had been convicted of a criminal offence three times since the age of sixteen. Sentences ranged from five to ten years.

Just as juvenile courts had grown informally prior to the passage of legislation so, similarly, arrangements for the supervision of offenders within the community also existed before the Probation of Offenders Act 1908. Young people formed by far the majority of probationers, and by 1920 80 per cent of the 10,000 people under probation supervision were under 21 (Rutherford, 1986). Although the Great War shifted attention away from penal policy there was, within a few years of the outbreak of war, a significant increase in recorded juvenile crime – from approximately 37,000 juveniles charged in 1913 to over 50,000 in 1917 – and some consequent congestion in the reformatories and industrial schools (Bailey, 1987).

By the early 1920s there was also some public disquiet following media allegations of brutality in a number of the borstal institutions. In January 1925 a Home Office Departmental Committee on the Treatment of Young Offenders (the Molony Committee) was set up. The terms of reference of the committee were wide, being to look into the treatment of young offenders under 21 and those who as a result of poor surroundings were in need of 'protection and training'. The Committee favoured the retention of the juvenile court and recommended that magistrates should be given the fullest possible information about those who appeared before them, including their home circumstances and their educational and medical histories (Morris and Giller, 1987). The focus at this time, then, was firmly upon the 'welfare' of young offenders and the 'treatment' necessary to reclaim or reform them.

The principle that young people were not only to be dealt with separately from adults but in a way that promoted their welfare was also to be found in the Children and Young Persons Act 1933. The 1933 Act incorporated much of what the Molony Committee had to say concerning those up to the age of 17^5, though it did not bar 16 year-olds from borstal as the committee had recommended. It did, however, give legislative effect to what had become administrative practice by prohibiting capital punishment for those under the age of eighteen.

In 1936 the maximum age for a borstal sentence was raised from 20 to 21, and these institutions constituted the only expanding part of the prison system in the inter-war years. There had been a sea-change during this period: prison numbers had declined, institutions closed, probation thrived and, as one later report claimed, 'in a variety of ways... Britain became the centre of the prison reform movement' (Home Office 1979, quoted in Windlesham, 1993).

Between 1938 and 1945 recorded indictable offences rose by 69 per cent, and before long the prison population began to swell, and the increase in juvenile crime exposed the difficulties inherent in a system dependent on accommodation provided by charities and local authorities. In 1942 the Home Secretary, Herbert Morrison, began to push for the establishment of a committee on penal reform. Eventually in 1944 an Advisory Council on the Treatment of Offenders under the Chairmanship of Mr Justice Birkett was set up. The post-war Labour government embarked on an extensive programme of legislation and a Criminal Justice Bill was introduced in 1947. It was heavily based on recommendations made before the war[6] which 'strongly emphasised the unwisdom of sending young persons to prison' (quoted in Bailey, 1987) and, indeed, the 1948 Act did place a number of restrictions on the use of imprisonment. It also introduced remand centres, attendance centres, support for probation hostels and abolished corporal punishment. However, the Magistrates' Association had renewed their demands for a new short-term custodial sentence and this was eventually accepted by the Labour Government. The Home Secretary, Chuter Ede, told the House of Commons:

> there is a type of offender to whom it is necessary to give a short, but sharp reminder that he is getting into ways that will inevitably lead him into disaster... their regime will consist of brisk discipline and hard work (quoted in Rutherford, 1986).

The detention centre order introduced by the 1948 Act was intended to be a short unpleasant sentence which would combine hard work with the minimum of amusement – a sentence not unlike the 'short, sharp, shock' experiment of the early 1980s.

Although there was considerable continuity between the Criminal Justice Bill of 1938 and the 1948 Act, there were also significant differences. Thus, although in 1938 a Conservative Home Secretary rejected the idea of detention centres, a decade later his Labour successor accepted the idea. Indeed, the provision passed through parliament with the minimum of debate, as most eyes were directed towards proposals to abolish capital and corporal punishment (Dunlop and McCabe, 1965; Windlesham, 1993). As will be clear from this discussion, the 1948 Act was far from being an entirely punitive piece of legislation, and the continuing concern about the 'welfare' of juveniles also found expression in the Children Act passed in the same year. Influenced by a report from the Care of Children Committee, the Children Act 1948 sought to end the placement of neglected children in approved schools alongside offenders, and to that end set up local authority children's departments with their own resources for residential care and trained staff to oversee fostering and adoption, thereby creating 'the first professional social work service exclusively for children' (Harris and Webb, 1987).

The post-war period was characterised by a continued rise in recorded juvenile crime, and it was increasingly suggested that the approved school system was unable to cope with some of the hardened young offenders that were coming before the courts (although provision for detention centres was included in the 1948 Criminal Justice Act, the first of these institutions was not opened until 1952[7]). As Windlesham (1993) has argued, from this point on 'the twin claws of the pincer that was to hold the development of penal policy fast in its grip were the remorseless increase in the incidence of crime, and the overcrowding in the prisons'.

The 1950s closed with the Ingleby committee which was set up in 1956 to inquire into the operation of the juvenile court. In its report of 1960 the committee endorsed the structure of the juvenile court, and it rejected any merger of approved schools with other residential accommodation or the removal of responsibility for these institutions from the Home Office. At least one commentator has suggested that a close reading of the report suggests that the committee favoured the development of a local-authority-based system of social service based on the children's departments established in 1948 as a method of decriminalising juvenile justice (Stevenson, 1989). The major focus of the committee's deliberations centred on the conflict that it felt existed between the *judicial* and *welfare* functions of the juvenile court. This, it suggested resulted in:

> ...a child being charged with a petty theft or other wrongful act for which most people would say that no great penalty should be imposed, and the case apparently ending in a disproportionate sentence. For when the court causes enquiries to be made... the court may determine that the welfare of the child requires some very substantial interference which may amount to taking the child away from his home for a prolonged period.

The solution proposed by the committee was immediately to raise the age of criminal responsibility from 8 to 12 'with the possibility of it becoming 13 or 14' (Morris and Giller, 1987), and below that age only welfare proceedings could be brought. The major proposals did not become law – the Children and Young Persons Act 1963, by way of compromise, raised the age of criminal responsibility to 10 – although one author in particular has argued that they were of considerable symbolic importance to later events (Bottoms, 1974).

The Ingleby Report polarised the two main political parties over the issue of juvenile justice. The Labour Party welcomed its proposal with regard to age of criminal responsibility, but was critical of what it took to be the Committee's timidity, and in response set up its own inquiry under the chairmanship of Lord Longford. This inquiry recommended the total abolition of the juvenile courts on the basis that 'no child in early adolescence should have to face criminal proceedings: these children should receive the kind of treatment they need without any stigma' (quoted in Bottoms, 1974). The alternative was non-judicial consultation between the child, the child's parents and a newly formed 'family service'. The Longford Report was followed by a White Paper *The Child, The Family and the Young Offender* which reproduced much of Longford, including proposals to establish family councils and family courts, and to abolish the juvenile courts. On this occasion, with legislation a significant possibility, the proposals were vehemently attacked by lawyers, magistrates and probation officers (Bottoms, 1974). With its small parliamentary majority to protect, the Labour government withdrew the proposals (Clarke, 1980).

Three years later a second White Paper *Children in Trouble* was published and this, after some relatively minor amendments, found legislative embodiment in the *Children and Young Persons Act 1969* (CYPA 69). The juvenile court was retained (the proposal for a family court did not reappear), but the intention signalled by the White Paper was to increase the age of criminal responsibility to 14. Care was preferred over criminal proceedings; the circumstances under which court proceedings were possible was to be narrowed. Thus, 'care and protection' proceedings could be instituted for children between 10-14, but only when it could 'be established that the child was not receiving such care, protection and guidance as a good parent might reasonably be expected to give' (Morris and Giller, 1987). Juveniles between 14-17 could be subject to criminal proceedings but it was to be necessary in future for the police to consult with the local authority children's department before making an application to a magistrate. The intention was that the juvenile court should become a welfare-providing agency but also 'an agency of last resort' (Rutter and Giller, 1983).

It was also intended that detention centres and borstals for juveniles would be phased out and replaced by a new form of intervention – intermediate treatment. 'This [though] was less a policy of decarceration than a reiteration of the traditional welfare abhorrence of the prison system'

(Rutherford, 1986). Between the passage of the 1969 Act and the putative date for its implementation there was, once again, a change of government and the new Conservative administration announced that it would not be implementing significant sections of the legislation. The consequence was that juvenile courts continued to function pretty much as they had before: criminal proceedings for 10-14 year-olds continued, powers in relation to 14-16 year-olds were not restricted, and the minimum age for qualification for a borstal sentence was not increased. Perhaps most significantly, although care proceedings on the commission of an offence were made possible, such powers were used exceedingly sparingly, and the more traditional 'punitive' disposals were used increasingly by the juvenile courts during the 1970s – the number of custodial sentences, for example, rising from 3,000 in 1970 to over 7,000 in 1978 (Rutter and Giller, 1983; Cavadino and Dignan, 1992). Indeed, this general trend led one group of commentators[8] to argue that:

> The tragedy that has occurred since (the passage of the 1969 Act) can be best described as a situation in which the worst of all possible worlds came into existence – people have been persistently led to believe that the juvenile criminal justice system has become softer and softer, while the reality has been that it has become harder and harder (Thorpe et al, 1980, quoted in Muncie, 1984).

Despite the fact that it was only partly implemented, the CYPA69 became the scapegoat for all the perceived ills of juvenile crime and juvenile justice in the 1970s, and Rutherford (1986) has cast doubt on the extent to which practice actually changed. He has suggested that it was 'the ideas and attitudes... culminating in the 1969 Act... on which the campaign for counter-reform was mounted'. The Act was attacked from all sides, not just by those critical of its 'welfare' elements, and within three years of its implementation a sub-committee of the House of Commons Expenditure Committee had been set up to make recommendations for change. The omens were not good, however, for:

> ...the inquiry was based on the assumption that the Act was not working although no evidence was quoted in favour of this. The membership of the Committee included at least two former magistrates and one former manager of an approved school, but nobody with close working or personal connections with the social work profession or social services departments (Farrington, 1984).

Although treatment and welfare had been heralded as the basis for progress from the late 1960s onwards, the legislative platform on which such a programme might have been built was never properly constructed. The Expenditure Committee, while accepting that there was a class of juvenile that required care and support rather than punishment, nevertheless was much influenced by the view that there was also, as the Magistrates' Association put it in their evidence:

> a minority of tough sophisticated young criminals... [who]... prey on the community, at will, even after the courts have placed them in care. They deride the powerlessness of the courts to do anything effective (quoted in Rutherford, 1986).[9]

This statement, one should note, bears more than a passing resemblance to much of what is currently being said about so-called 'persistent juvenile offenders'.

As a consequence, the Committee argued that it was important to

> hasten the process in the case of certain offenders to deter others from embarking on criminal activities, to contain a hard core of *persistent offenders*, and to punish some offenders (House of Commons Expenditure Committee, 1975, quoted in Morris and Giller, 1987, emphasis added).

The aim of the Committee was, then, to make some form of distinction between children who need care and those who in their words require 'strict control and an element of punishment', and it was critical of the 1969 Act for not doing so, even though the Act deliberately attempted to obscure such boundaries.

In response the government issued a White Paper[10] which was ambivalent in its views of juvenile justice, both recommending a shift away from residential care and towards supervision and fostering, whilst also sharing

> the widespread anxiety that is felt... about the continuing problem of how to cope with a small minority, among delinquent children, of serious and persistent offenders. It is in this area... that the present measures under the Act are felt to be falling short (Home Office et al., 1976, para.3).

Though it did not attempt to define how this hard core of persistent juvenile offenders might be distinguished from the majority, it nevertheless signalled the intention to establish different strategies and systems for dealing with each.

It is hard not to agree with Morris' and Giller's (1987) conclusion that juvenile justice policy at the end of the 1970s 'bore little resemblance to that proposed in the 1969 Act.' In particular, they suggest, the police and the Magistrates' Association had been successful in establishing their model of 'juvenile delinquency' as the dominant one in operation in the juvenile justice system. Responsibility for the 'persistent juvenile offenders' that they identified as the core of the problem was increasingly placed in the hands of local authority social services departments. A joint working party on persistent juvenile offending that included representatives of the magistracy and local authorities reported in 1978, but failed to agree on how the problem should be tackled, the Magistrates' Association continuing to press for short detention centre orders, a demand that was being echoed by William Whitelaw, the Shadow Home Secretary, who by this stage was calling for the introduction of 'short, sharp, shock' treatment (Harwin, 1982).

The Conservative manifesto of 1979 had promised to strengthen sentencing powers with respect to juveniles and young adults and the 1980 White Paper, *Young Offenders*, included proposals for the reintroduction of a limited number of detention centres with 'tougher' regimes, and this 'experiment' began in two centres – Send and New Hall – in 1980. The subsequent *Criminal Justice Act 1982* shortened the detention centre sentence: its minimum and maximum lengths were reduced from three and six months to 21 days and four months (Cavadino and Dignan, 1992). Imprisonment for under-21s was abolished and the end of the road for borstals was signalled with the new order for 'youth custody' (the institutions becoming known as youth custody centres). The youth custody order was a determinate sentence whose length was fixed by the sentencing court (though with the possibility of remission and parole). The minimum youth custody sentence was four months and one day, and magistrates and juvenile courts could impose sentences between the minimum and six months, and the government's intention was that the shorter (though 'sharper') sentence, together with a requirement that sentencers should impose a custodial sentence only if they were satisfied that no other alternative was possible[11], would reduce the number of juveniles held in custody (discussed in *Young Offenders*, 1980, para.46). There was considerable scepticism in some quarters, however, at the extent to which the government was committed to the use of community-based alternatives to imprisonment, and there were fears that custodial institutions would become ever more central in juvenile justice (Allen, 1991). The late 1970s had seen the abandonment of the philosophy contained in the CYPA 69, a decline in the use of community-based penalties for juvenile offenders and a corresponding increase in the use of custody. Morris and Giller (1987) quote a DHSS review of sentencing trends in the juvenile court which found that the proportion of 14-17 year-olds referred to the court that received custodial penalties had increased from 1 in 800 in 1965 to 1 in 180 by 1979. Moreover, the review (DHSS, 1981) suggested that only one sixth of this increase could be explained by reference to changes in juvenile crime.

Figure 1.1   Males aged 14-16 sentenced to custody, 1971-1990

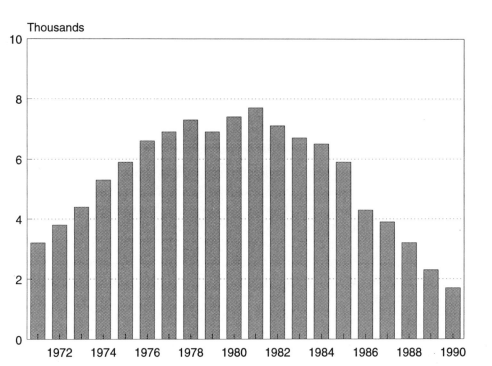

Unlikely as it might seem against this background, a significant and sustained decline in the use of custody for juveniles during the 1980s is exactly what happened (see Figure 1.1). As Rutherford (1986) commented, the paradox is that 'the decade of "law and order" was also the decade of what has been called "the successful revolution" in juvenile justice'. One former Home Office minister has described this transformation as 'one of the most remarkable post-war achievements of deliberate legislative enactment' (Windlesham, 1993), and seen against the backdrop of 'evolution, revolution and counter-revolution' in juvenile justice (Morris and Giller, 1987) described above, it is impossible to deny that it is indeed a remarkable achievement. The extent to which it may be attributed to deliberate legislative enactment is, however, somewhat more debatable.

In the first instance, although it cannot explain the full extent of the fall in numbers, there were significant demographic changes during this period that must be taken into account. There was, for example, a 17 per cent decline in the number of males in the 14-16 age group between 1981-88. Furthermore, in the same period the number of young people sentenced also decreased by about 38 per cent. The success of the general policy of 'diverting' juveniles from prosecution meant that there were far fewer candidates for custodial sentences. In addition to the policy of diversion from prosecution, it seems likely that fewer of those who did come before the courts received custodial sentences. The 1982 Criminal Justice Act had placed new restrictions on judicial discretion in relation to the use of custody and extended the range of non-custodial options.

One of the keys to diversion was the increased use of cautioning by the police. The 1980 White Paper had accepted that

> juvenile offenders who can be diverted from the criminal justice system at an early stage in their offending are less likely to reoffend than those who become involved in judicial proceedings (para. 3.8).

The police clearly have great discretion in dealing with offenders, particularly with young offenders and, indeed, successive research studies have shown that there are marked variations in the use of cautioning between police forces (Tutt and Giller, 1983; Laycock and Tarling, 1985; Evans and Wilkinson, 1990). A series of Home Office Circulars (in 1978, 1985 and 1990) encouraged the police to use their power to caution. The 14/1985 Circular issued to chief constables included criteria to be applied by the police with the aim of increasing the likelihood of diversion from prosecution and the 1990 Circular included national standards and also, though it suggested they should be used sparingly, recognised the possible use of 'multiple cautions': it countenanced 'offenders being cautioned more than once, provided the nature and circumstances of the most recent offence warrant it'.

Alongside the increase in the use of cautioning there were also changes in the use of non-custodial penalties – diversion once again, this time from custody rather than prosecution[12]. The 1982 Act introduced new requirements that could be attached to supervision orders (Graham and Moxon, 1986). The following year, the DHSS issued a Circular LAC 83(3) in which it announced that £15 million was to be provided to support intensive intermediate treatment (IT) programmes as an alternative to custody. Monitoring by NACRO of the subsequent development of schemes suggests that this initiative may also have had some impact on the custodial sentencing of juveniles (NACRO, 1987), though the forthcoming results of more substantial research conducted by the Cambridge Institute of Criminology may qualify such a finding.

In addition to announcing the funding, LAC 83(3) also recommended that work with serious and persistent young offenders should be coordinated by inter-agency committees. Subsequently, such committees or panels have been formed, often involving sentencers as well as representatives of other relevant agencies. One of the consequences of this, it has been argued

(NACRO, 1989), has been to provide a first step towards a more integrated system of juvenile justice (Allen, 1991).

In addition to the decline in the number of juveniles sentenced to custody during the latter part of the 1980s there was also a shift in the use of detention centre and youth custody sentences. In the aftermath of the 1982 Act magistrates took the opportunity to use their new powers to send juveniles to youth custody centres and were much less attracted to the new 'short, sharp, shock' detention centre regimes. In fact the experiment was, largely, a failure; evaluation by the Home Office's Young Offender Psychology Unit concluded that the new regimes seemed to be no more effective than the previous ones. More than half of those sent to detention centres had been reconvicted within a year, irrespective of the type of regime in the centre at which they served their sentence (Home Office, 1984). Despite this, the experiment was, briefly, extended to all detention centres, though aspects of the regime were modified. 'The political damage was limited' suggests Windlesham (1993), 'but it is hard to avoid the verdict that sound penal administration was made to serve the needs of a defective icon of political ideology'.

In the longer term the government decided to abolish the separate detention centre sentence. The Criminal Justice Act 1988 included a new sentence of 'detention in a young offender institution', and separate detention centres ceased to exist, being amalgamated with youth custody centres to become young offender institutions (YOIs). Courts were given the power to decide on the length of sentence though where the sentence was to be served was to be determined by the Home Office. Detention in a YOI is available for people aged 15 and above.

Before moving on it is important to mention the existence, and demise, of the s.7(7) care order. This was an order created by the CYPA 69, which could be used by the juvenile court in criminal proceedings to place a juvenile in the care of the local authority. The local authority then placed the juvenile where it thought most appropriate, including back in the parental home. During the 1970s, practice in relation to care orders was criticised by magistrates on the one hand for tending to undermine the intentions of the court by failing to place offenders where they could be controlled and, on the other hand, by academic critics concerned at the potential criminogenic consequences of using a care order early on in an offender's 'career' (see, for example, Thorpe et al, 1980). Significant claims have been made about the impact of this academic critique (Cavadino and Dignan, 1992) though, whatever the reality, the use of s.7(7) care orders declined rapidly during the 1980s and they were eventually abolished (from October 1991) by the Children Act 1989.

For the purposes of this discussion here, there is one final significant change that has taken place in juvenile justice since that point. The Criminal Justice Act 1991 changed the name of the Juvenile Court to the Youth Court and extended its jurisdiction to include 17 year-olds. The clear aim was to extend the gains made with the younger age group to 17 year-olds and, indeed, as early as 1988 in the Green Paper *Punishment, Custody and the Community*, the Home Office signalled its intention to transfer the lessons learnt in juvenile justice to policies in relation to offenders more generally, though it recognised that modifications would need to be made (Home Office, 1988, paras, 2.17-19). It did, however, emphasise the reasons for seeking to restrict the use of custodial sentences for young offenders:

> most young offenders grow out of crime as they become more mature and responsible. They need encouragement and help to become law abiding. Even a short period of custody is quite likely to confirm them as criminals, particularly as they acquire new criminal skills from the more sophisticated offenders. They see themselves labelled as criminals and behave accordingly.

The 1991 Criminal Justice Act, in tandem with the Children Act 1989 which was part of the same general development (Faulkner, 1992), continued the by now well-established twin-track approach of punishment and welfare. The Children Act 1989 gave statutory recognition to the need to avoid prosecution, and the 1991 Act and subsequent Home Office Circular (30/92) that explained the changes brought about by the legislation reminded sentencers of s.44 of the Children and Young Persons Act 1933 which states that 'all courts must have regard to the welfare of children and young people who appear before them'. The Act extended this consideration to 17 year-olds. The legislation also gave magistrates new sentencing powers within the overall framework created by the 1991 Act (including unit fines, community sentences and custody[13]) along with a new scheme of post-custody supervision. The Act reduced the maximum term of detention in a YOI to 12 months, and brought 17 year-olds within the ambit of s.53 of the Children and Young Persons Act 1933 which gives the Crown Court the power to order longer terms of detention in respect of certain 'grave crimes'. Finally, again reinforcing lessons learnt from developments in practice over the past decade, the 1991 Act signalled the importance of inter-agency and joint working by giving Chief Probation Officers and Directors of Social Services joint responsibility for making local arrangements to provide services to the Youth Court.

Persistent offending

The history of juvenile justice, though relatively short, is an extremely complicated one. It has been characterised by the coexisting approaches of 'welfare' and 'punishment': a tendency on the one hand to wish to support and protect those children who for a variety of reasons may find themselves on the wrong side of the law and, on the other hand, a determination to ensure that those who continually offend despite efforts to stop them receive a punishment that makes clear that their behaviour is unacceptable. The tension between these two approaches is seen at its starkest in the debates over how best to respond to that 'hardcore' of young people whose offending, it is believed, continues unchecked irrespective of the interventions of criminal justice agencies.

This, then, is the background against which the most recent rise in concern about juvenile offending, and *persistent* offending in particular, has developed. The concern about juvenile offending, though something which is to an extent ever-present in our society, was fuelled by very specific factors in the early 1990s. The first of these was the well-publicised urban disturbances of 1991. Though they were not on the scale or, indeed, similar in their causes or style to the riots of the early 1980s, the disturbances at Blackbird Leys (Oxford), Ely (Cardiff) and on the Meadowell estate in Tyneside focused attention on young men in large-scale violent confrontations with the police, in many cases as a consequence of attempts by the latter to put a stop to the very public displays of 'joyriding' so popular with young men and with the journalists who increasingly turned up to report their activities (Campbell, 1993).

From mid-1991 onwards stories started to appear in the press about youngsters who, it was believed, were so involved in crime that they accounted for a significant proportion of juvenile crime in the areas in which they lived. It was suggested that the police and courts were powerless to deal with these offenders. The issue was taken up in a speech to the Federated Ranks of the Metropolitan Police in October 1992 by the then Home Secretary, Kenneth Clarke. A small number of children, he suggested,

> are committing a large number of crimes. There is a case for increasing court powers to lock up, educate and train them for their own and everyone else's interest. We will certainly be taking a long hard look at the options which are available to the courts in dealing with serious offenders of this age. If court powers need to be strengthened or new institutions created, then they will be.

Public concern about the level of juvenile crime and the perceived ineffectiveness of the criminal justice system to deal with the problem remained high in the following months, and in early March 1993, Mr Clarke announced that the government proposed to introduce legislation that would make a new disposal available to the courts. These 'secure training orders', were to be aimed at 'that comparatively small group of very persistent juvenile offenders whose repeated offending makes them a menace to the community' (HC Deb 2 March 1993, col.139).

The new order would apply to 12-15 year-olds who had been convicted of three imprisonable offences, and who had proved 'unwilling or unable to comply with the requirements of supervision in the community while on remand or under sentence'. The order was to be a custodial one of up to two years and would be served in a 'secure training unit' which, he suggested, would provide 'high standards of care and discipline'. Regimes would include provision for education and training for inmates; after release, individuals would be subject to 'rigorous, consistent and firmly delivered' supervision until their supervising social worker or probation officer felt that he or she was no longer a threat to society.

Earlier, in the Autumn of 1992, the House of Commons Home Affairs Committee (HAC) had announced that it would be inquiring into issues affecting juvenile offenders and the particular problems of persistent offenders. In explaining its reasons for doing so the Committee said: 'We decided on this inquiry both because of public concern about the level of juvenile crime in particular, and because of the apparent inability of the criminal justice system to deal adequately with it' (HAC, 1993).

Given what has been said above about recent trends in juvenile crime – a relatively sharp decline in recorded juvenile crime during the 1980s and early 1990s – it is worth briefly considering what the Home Affairs Committee made of the fact that there existed significant 'public concern about the level of juvenile crime'. The Committee received much evidence which backed up the picture presented by official criminal statistics of a general decline of *recorded* juvenile crime, set against a background of significant increases in recorded crime overall. The word 'recorded' is important here, for a number of witnesses made much of the fact that the same period may well have seen a significant rise in the use of informal warnings by the police (sometimes referred to as informal cautions), and that because such warnings are not recorded, they may account, at least in part, for some of the divergence between what official statistics suggested and what the public and politicians felt.

In addition, evidence was presented by the Association of Chief Police Officers (ACPO) which suggested that, given the decline in the juvenile population during the 1980s, the increase in crime more generally and the generally reduced rate of detection, the period from 1980 to 1990 had in fact witnessed a 54 per cent rise in juvenile crime. Indeed, they were given some support from the Shadow Home Secretary and one of the Shadow Home Affairs Ministers who also suggested that it was 'difficult to believe Home Office claims that offending by young people has actually gone down across the country' (HAC, 1993, para 7). The Home Affairs Committee in seeking an explanation for this apparent disagreement suggested that it was in part due to the fact that the official criminal statistics referred to numbers of offenders whereas ACPO were referring to the number of offences. As ACPO then said, whilst it did not challenge the proposition that the number of known juvenile offenders had fallen, that is not the same as saying 'that the amount of crime committed by juveniles has not increased'. The Home Affairs Committee was, not unnaturally, unable to resolve the issue, but it did suggest that:

> one possible explanation for the apparent discrepancy between ACPOs picture of greater juvenile offending and the decline in the number of juvenile offenders is a growth in the numbers of *persistent* offenders... If there is a small but growing number of juvenile offenders responsible for many offences (some of which they may be convicted or cautioned for and some of which may go undetected) it is possible to reconcile the indisputable fact that the number (and rate, to a lesser extent) of known juvenile offenders has fallen over time with the more speculative assertion that the number of offences committed by juveniles has risen. (HAC, 1993, para.15)

Having identified this possibility, the Home Affairs Committee then went on to consider the issue of persistent offending and received a generally uniform picture from the majority of agencies. ACPO, for example, talked of a 'small hard core who have absolutely no fears whatsoever of the criminal justice system', and continued, 'society is entitled to expect a degree of protection from the ravages of the persistent juvenile offender'. Although there were few other witnesses quite so certain in their descriptions, there were few who took exception to the idea that there existed a small group of offenders that might, as the Home Affairs Committee put it, be described as 'persistent juvenile trouble makers'. The Committee went on:

> the Association of Chief Officers of Probation (ACOP) told us that there might be, for example, 10-12 such individuals in Hampshire, while NAPO suggested that there were 12-20 in Newcastle. This may only be, as ACOP said, 'a very, very small handful', but there is clearly a significant group of individuals country-wide who cause a disproportionate amount of the crime attributed to young people.

The study reported below follows on from work undertaken by the Home Office itself focusing on the persistent offender. In a small-scale·

study, police forces were asked by the Home Office to provide data on all the juveniles in their jurisdiction who were known or believed to have committed 10 or more offences in a specified three-month period during 1992 (April to June). Thirty-three police forces responded to the request, and were able to identify juveniles in their area that met these criteria, and between them they identified a total of 106 juveniles. The maximum number of persistent juvenile offenders in any one police force area was 14. The definition included offences that had been 'taken into consideration' by a court, and those that resulted in no further action by the police. The police completed questionnaires concerning the age, sex, and ethnic origin of the offenders, as well as characteristics of the offences, including the date it was committed, the type of offence and the outcome. Burglary, theft of cars, theft from cars and theft from shops accounted for the majority of offences committed. Assault accounted for approximately 1 per cent of the total offences. Nearly a third of the offences were committed whilst the offender was on bail. In approximately a third of the cases, the result was that the offender was charged or summonsed, and 7.5 per cent were convicted. Over a third of offences were taken into consideration by the court when the offender was being prosecuted for other offences.

The accuracy and reliability of the research were disputed by several of the witnesses to the Home Affairs Committee, who generally took the view that it was probably an underestimate of the true incidence of persistent offenders – a view accepted by the Home Office. The reality, as a recent report from The National Children's Home (NCH, 1993) suggested, is that there is little rigorous information available about the extent of 'persistent' offending and, consequently, much discussion about how best to respond to this problem is based on anecdote and assertion, and there is little or no agreement on how such offending should be defined. Indeed, finding a definition for 'persistence' has been a problem for those few research studies in this area that have been attempted previously.

Wolfgang et al (1972) used *number of arrests* as the method of distinguishing what they referred to as 'chronic offenders'. In their study – a follow-up of nearly 10,000 boys – they suggested that the 'chronic offenders' (those with five or more arrests each) represented 6.3 per cent of the cohort and accounted for over half of the total number of arrests for the whole group. An approximately similar finding was reported by West and Farrington (1977), though their threshold was six or more convictions. It is generally established therefore that a small proportion of young offenders account for a disproportionately large number of juvenile arrests and convictions (see also Home Office Statistical Department, 1985;

Farrington, 1987). Consequently, it is felt that concentrating the attentions of the criminal justice system on this group might be particularly worthwhile. As Tarling (1993) has argued,

> if the small group of chronic offenders could be identified early in their criminal careers and targeted for some form of successful intervention to reduce their offending this could have a significant impact on crime.

Are these offenders distinguishable from the majority? The little research evidence that exists suggests that the differences between the 'chronic' and other offenders are merely differences of degree. The research by Wadsworth (1979), West (1982), Ouston (1984) and Blumstein et al (1985) all identify factors such as low IQ, low family income, low school achievement, a history of offending in the family and so on, but also show that such factors also distinguish offenders from non-offenders. The ability to predict those offenders who will be chronic offenders and those who will not is, therefore, somewhat limited[14]. Nevertheless, interest in this small group of high-rate offenders remains high, and it is they who are the focus of the research reported in the following chapters. The question of how 'persistence' might be defined is one of the key themes running throughout this report.

Notes

1. The 'standard list' is a group of offences that includes all indictable offences and a small number of summary offences, but which excludes that majority of minor, mainly motoring, offences.

2. Prior to the Criminal Justice Act 1991, 'juvenile' referred to young people aged between 10 and 16 years of age. The 1991 Act extended the definition to include 17 year olds. However, it also changed the name of the Juvenile Court to the Youth Court, with the consequence that these young people are now generally referred to as young offenders rather than juvenile offenders. There is currently some confusion about how this group of offenders should be described, and where possible we have used the term 'young offender'. There remain some occasions where juvenile offender and juvenile offending seem more appropriate.

3. Though there is some dispute about how 'similarly' adults and children were really treated by the criminal justice system, cf. Platt (1978).

4. The Reformatory Schools Act 1854.

5. In fact the committee's proposals were given statutory force by the Children and Young Person's Act 1932 which was consolidated by the 1933 Act.

6. Recommendations originally contained in the *Young Offenders Report* 1927, and later in the 1938 Criminal Justice Bill.

7. Provision for (Senior) Attendance Centres was also included in the 1948 Act but it was a full decade before they came into being. For a full history see Mair, G. (1991).

8. These authors who, themselves, advocated an approach to juvenile justice known as 'systems management', 'can claim a substantial degree of success' according to Cavadino and Dignan (1992). The authors were critical of traditional welfarism which they argued failed, despite its best efforts, to limit the degree of state social control over juvenile offenders.

9. Rutherford (1986) quotes two further members of the Association expressing similar views: 'Sir William Addison talked of "the hard core of young offenders – that is to say, the offenders in the youngest age group – that is now resulting in the very serious increase in the incidence of crime in the 15 to 17 age groups". Mr RC Stranger added: "the hard core of sophisticated young criminals hitherto considered and spoken of as small in number but which one fears [is] increasing".'

10. Home Office and others (1976).

11. S.1(4) of the Criminal Justice Act 1982 laid down that a young offender could be sentenced to custody only if the court was satisfied that one of the following three conditions was met: (a) that the offender was unable or unwilling to respond to non-custodial penalties; (b) that custody was necessary for the protection of the public; or (c) that the offence was so serious that a non-custodial penalty could not be justified. (The criteria were subsequently amended by the Criminal Justice Act 1988 and eventually superseded by the new criteria in the Criminal Justice Act 1991 which also apply to adults.)

12. This is not to ignore the quite extended debate that has taken place about the possibility that some of these changes – increased use of cautioning and non-custodial penalties for example – may have resulted in a degree of 'net-widening', ie bringing into the criminal justice process children who would not otherwise have been there (cf. Ditchfield, 1976; Farrington and Bennett, 1981; Giller and Tutt, 1987).

13. The 1993 Criminal Justice Act amended some of the provisions of the 1991 Act, including abolishing unit fines.

14. For a full discussion of the techniques and the difficulties involved, see Tarling, 1993. See also Farrington and West (1993) who provide recent evidence on the possibility of differences between chronic and non-chronic offenders.

2 Method of Research

Overview

This study of juvenile offending concentrates on offenders who have been arrested several times. By so doing, it concentrates on the more extreme end of juvenile offending. A large proportion of young offenders will be arrested once or twice and then cease offending, or cease to be arrested, (Home Office, 1985; Knight and West, 1975). A smaller proportion will go on to be arrested several times, and those under investigation in this study were arrested three times or more within one calendar year, which makes them relatively unusual. Figures presented by Laycock and Tarling (1985) suggest that, taking a summary measure of the number of arrests that resulted in a caution or a prosecution for a sample of 5,000 offenders born in 1963, only 17.5 per cent will have been arrested three times or more as juveniles. As our criterion was arrests within one calendar year, it is likely that this group of reoffenders form a very small proportion of all young offenders.

The research was conducted in two geographical areas. The first was a Midlands county; the second consisted of two London boroughs, combined to provide a large enough sample of London juveniles arrested three times or more. In the remainder of this report, these juveniles will be referred to as *young reoffenders.* The focus of the study was on 10 to 16 year olds and in each area, all juveniles (under 17 years old[1]) were identified who, according to police records, had been arrested three times or more in 1992. This produced a total of 552 young people. Twenty-one people were excluded at this stage either because their police files were unavailable at the time of data collection, probably because other police officers were using them, or because examination of their files revealed that they were actually outside the age range. There remained a pool of 531 young offenders aged between 10 and 16 at the beginning of 1992.

Subsequently, data on these 531 offenders were collected from three different sources. Figure 2.1 presents a schematic portrait of the study design. This demonstrates the nature of the multiple sources of data that were accessed in order to develop a picture of young reoffenders in these two geographical areas. Police files on all 531 young offenders were read,

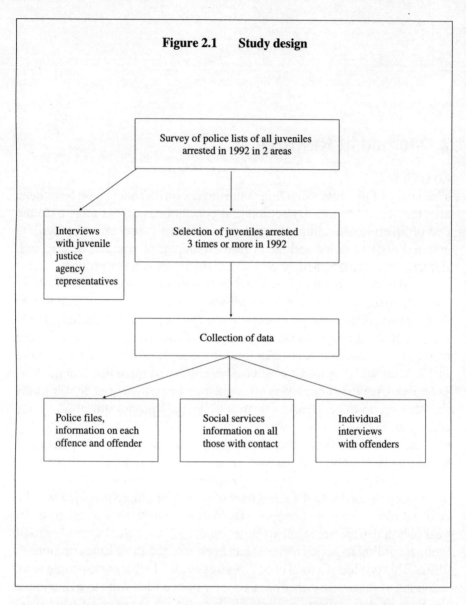

Figure 2.1   Study design

Survey of police lists of all juveniles arrested in 1992 in 2 areas

Interviews with juvenile justice agency representatives

Selection of juveniles arrested 3 times or more in 1992

Collection of data

Police files, information on each offence and offender

Social services information on all those with contact

Individual interviews with offenders

and social services information was collected on those of the 531 children who were known to the social services departments in their areas. In addition, attempts were made to trace and interview approximately half of the offenders (251), and 74 were fully interviewed. Further details on each of these stages of data collection will be presented below.

There were four main reasons why this study design was chosen.

♦ Primarily, the design was appropriate because it involved random selection from the general population of young reoffenders. Thus, it allowed us to focus on larger numbers of offenders only, as the sampling excluded non-offenders. More importantly, it allowed us to focus on those who were coming to the attention of the police relatively frequently, unlike, for example, the Cambridge Study of Delinquency or other cohort studies which do not include very many high-rate offenders.

There is one important caveat to enter at this point. The sample was selected from lists of arrestees kept by the police. Hence, it consists of only those reoffenders who come to the attention of, and who are arrested by, the police. Whilst this potentially biases the sample in one respect, there were important reasons for taking this approach. As this was to include a study of persistent young offenders who are said to be a particular problem for the police and the courts, it seemed reasonable to focus upon those who had come to the attention of the police. Those who had not come to notice could not, by definition, be a problem for the police or the courts. They might still, of course, be a problem for the communities in which they live, or for other agencies. It remains possible that those who do not get arrested are not particularly different from those that do, at least in terms of social and educational factors, alcohol and drug use, and other issues raised in this report. However, the longitudinal research evidence cited in the previous chapter suggests that this is unlikely (Blumstein et al, 1985). There is a need for further research investigating the differences between those who are known to the police and those who remain uncaught.

♦ The nature of the design allowed for mixture of data sources, minimising bias due to emphasis on one agency rather than another. This variety of data will lead to a more complete picture of the functioning of the juvenile justice system.

♦ The design mixed survey methodology with more in-depth methods. This allowed us to cover large numbers of offenders in some detail, and smaller numbers in much more detail. The combination gives a better idea of the extent and nature of persistent juvenile offendingthan reliance on one method only.

♦ This design enabled us to interview some of the young people themselves. Given that so little is known about juveniles who reoffend frequently, this was an important element of the research.

The three sources of information on young reoffenders
Police records

In both the Midlands county and the London boroughs, police information came from three distinct places. In the first instance, information was collected from police records in separate police stations (usually in the form of index cards or chronological lists of juveniles arrested in the area), including name(s)[2], sex, date(s) of birth, number of processed arrests in 1992, and criminal record number.

Second, each separate file on the juveniles selected was read at the central police headquarters for the region. In the London boroughs, these headquarters were the youth and community departments. In the Midlands, they were the force headquarters. These files contained information on all separate police contacts with the juveniles, with bundles of papers and police forms relating to each set of offences. Information in the files related both to offences that ended in prosecution and also those that were dropped at a fairly early stage. A sample recording form for collecting this information from the police files shows that information was collected on addresses, guardianship, ethnicity, 1992 offences, and 1992 court results (Appendix 1).

Finally, official recorded information on convictions was collected: in the Midlands this information was computerised; in London it was kept on microfiche and had to be requested from Central Records. This provided a double-check on the information collected in the separate files.

Social services records

In addition to information from the police records, data were also drawn from the social services records of the Midlands county and one of the London boroughs. The departments were provided with a list of all young reoffenders identified from police records and they then identified all those who had had any contact with social services throughout their lives.

Data collection from social services varied between the two areas, due to the nature of the social services databases. In the Midlands county, computerised records allowed relatively easy access to care histories for the juveniles. In the London borough, each social services file relating to a juvenile known to the department had to be read individually. Information was gathered from social services on whether or not the child was on the child protection register, the total number of episodes of social services care in the child's life, the number of episodes of care within 1992, details of dates of start and end of the first episode, the current episode and all 1992 episodes, and data on the type of placements provided by social services. 'Episodes' referred to the number of different periods in different places of accommodation (including the parental home) that the child had had whilst being looked after by the social services.

Interviews with juveniles

All juveniles arrested three times in the two London boroughs were selected for interviewing, together with a sample of juveniles from the Midlands county, where larger numbers had been identified. This gave a total of 251 juveniles for whom tracing and interviewing was attempted. Because of problems anticipated in seeing the more frequent reoffenders, the sample in the Midlands county was biased towards the more persistent offenders, in the hope that this would produce a full spread of respondents from all parts of the offending continuum. There were great difficulties in tracing individuals belonging to this highly unusual group. Altogether 74 were successfully interviewed. There were a total of 41 refusals from the 251 families where a reoffender was selected for interview; approximately half of these came from the reoffenders themselves and the remainder from family members. The rest of the young people (156) were untraced or uncontactable.

The interviews were set up and conducted by six interviewers (and the first author) and they took place between May and October 1993. Five of the six interviewers were young men, the sixth a young woman. All six were experienced interviewers, with backgrounds in psychology or criminology. Interviewers were instructed to maintain the structure of the interview schedule, but were encouraged to allow the interviewees to add comments and have general discussion.

Piloting clarified various issues about both the content of the interview schedule and the nature of our approach to the reoffenders and their families. For example, it was apparent from several of the pilot interviews that some members of the family were unaware of the extent of the child's arrests. For this reason, emphasis on the fact that the child had been arrested was reduced, in order to avoid provoking family arguments about previously unknown police contact.

The child's and parents' latest addresses were taken from police files and updated from social services information. The majority of the sample members were still under 18 years of age by the start of the interviewing period in the middle of 1993, and we began our approach by seeking parental permission, subsequently approaching the juveniles themselves. This had to be done for almost all children, including those in young offenders institutions, the only exceptions being those who were accommodated compulsorily by the local authority. The initial approach was by letter to the parent or guardian, followed by a visit by the interviewer, who explained the research project and asked the parent or guardian to sign a consent form, allowing us to ask the child whether or not he or she would like to take part. If the consent form was signed, attempts were made to trace and see the child. This was easiest in cases where the child was living with the parent. If he or she was not, addresses were either taken from the parents or, if they had no address for the child, attempts were made to trace the child independently, through other addresses on the police and social services files, other family members and telephone directories.

Interviewers told families and children that they were from the Policy Studies Institute, an independent research organisation interested in social issues, and that PSI was researching into juveniles and the criminal justice system. Frequently, people were interested in how PSI was financed, and interviewers explained that the funds came from a variety of sources including research foundations and government departments. Not surprisingly, they were equally interested in why their names had been picked, and the interviewer's introduction suggested that names and addresses were picked up from official files, generally police files. They avoided saying that names had been taken from lists of people who had been arrested, emphasising instead that they were talking to people who had had some kind of contact with the police over the last year or two. Confidentiality was stressed at all stages of the research, and it was suggested that one of the major elements of the study was a chance for teenagers to report their opinions and views on the police and the legal system, and on education, in order to improve the system for people of their age. Interviewers explained that they were interested in finding out about what sorts of things they felt worked and didn't work, what factors they felt meant that some people get into trouble and some don't, and what they thought about their futures.

A proportion of the reoffenders successfully interviewed were in some form of custody (7), or in children's homes (2). In the case of young offenders institutions (YOIs), when confirmation was available from the family or relatives that a reoffender was in custody, the governor of the YOI was approached and asked for permission to ask the young person to take part. In several cases, the YOIs themselves then sought further permission from parents for the research to take place. If and when the YOI, the teachers and the young person all agreed, interviewers visited the YOIs and conducted the interviews on the premises. To interview in children's homes, access was negotiated through social services district managers, the managers of the children's homes and, sometimes, the social worker and key residential worker, before seeking the cooperation of the child.

This description of the interviewing process gives an indication of the enormity of the task of seeking to interview these children, which in a large part explains the low response rate. The interview itself was well received and the respondents appeared to enjoy it. The problems lay in the process of getting to meet the child, and they took the following forms.

Finding the family Since we liaised with social services and the police to locate the family, the most problematic cases were those where the agencies themselves reported trouble in finding them. These families were fairly mobile, and – according to social services – increasingly so in the last few years. They did not leave forwarding addresses for precisely the reasons that we wanted to talk to them, for it was frequently several members of the family who were 'in trouble', not just our target child. They were often trying to keep a low profile from a number of different agencies including debt and council tax collectors. They rarely had telephones (or gave out their telephone number) and they changed their names frequently with changes in family formation.

Gaining the cooperation of the family The families were rarely antagonistic, but in a proportion of cases they would not allow us to meet the child, or ask the child to take part. In some cases, the person at the door refused, without revealing their relationship to the subject. On one occasion we received a letter from a solicitor, advising us that his client's father did not want us to contact the family. Several parents refused on the grounds that the child was trying 'to go clean' and they felt the interview would only make them think about offending again. This was never offered as reason for refusal by the young reoffenders themselves.

Finding the child after gaining parental permission The interviewers reported a striking lack of contact between the parents and the children. On visiting a house, after agreeing to come back another time, mothers would report 'he just hasn't been around'. In several cases where the families were happy for us to do the interview, they had no idea where the child was. It was not unusual for them to claim that they had not seen the child for a matter of months. In others cases, the child came home to sleep sometimes, but also lived at other (perhaps unknown) addresses. Within the older age group, they were sometimes in squats for part of the time; one was living in a mobile caravan.

Getting the child to be present at a particular time Even when the global cooperation of the child and family had been obtained, the child could still be remarkably elusive. In interview, one social services-based youth justice worker said that getting his young clients to turn up at an agreed time for an appointment was one of the major elements of his work.

'Their lives', he said, 'are just not geared to that sort of thing. If they had the ability to turn up on time, they wouldn't need me.'

Interviewing others

In addition to the three main sources of data outlined above, interviews were also conducted in the two study areas with representatives of the major criminal justice and welfare agencies (police officers, court clerks, magistrates, education and social workers), in order to provide background and context. These interviews focused on their understanding of the 'problem' of persistent offending by juveniles and their perceptions of the policy and current practices of their agency.

The juvenile interview schedule

The interview schedule developed for use with the reoffenders was a largely structured interview with a small proportion of open-ended questions. The emphasis was on collecting information about the child's current circumstances, and circumstances in 1992 if they had been different, the period that coincided with the information collected from official records. The interview took approximately 45 minutes to complete, and covered details of current living circumstances, current 'occupation', parental occupation and relationships with child, running away from home, contact with social services, educational background, truanting, attitudes to and influence of friends, self-reported offending, details of first arrest, perceptions of seriousness and risks of offending, perceptions of reasons for offending, physical health, alcohol and drug use, contact with psychological services, and perceptions of what the future might hold. A complete list of interview questions is contained in Appendix 2.

Administration of the self-report offending list

During the individual interviews with the subset of 74, offenders were asked to complete a self-report list of offences (see Appendix 3). The list was confidential, in that the interviewer handed over the list, stressed confidentiality, and asked the interviewee to complete it on his or her own. The interviewer then put the list, without looking at it, into an envelope. A number of these young people were not confident about their reading, and in these cases the interviewee was given the list, and the interviewer read the items in order from another copy. On occasion, the interviewees insisted on the interviewers filling in the list for them. The subjects did not appear to be threatened or secretive about the task, however the list was completed, and we are confident that the information is as accurate as self-reported offending is ever likely to be. A lot of care was taken to manage this exchange of information in a way that would maximise the freedom of the respondent, without encouraging them to over-report by providing any reaction or feedback.

Discussion of terms
Juveniles and young reoffenders
In this report, the term 'juvenile' refers to young people in the two study areas who were aged 10 years or over, and under 17, on 1 January 1992, the first day of the year over which their contact with the youth justice system was traced. The term 'young reoffender' refers to the children of the same age range who had been arrested and cautioned or charged three times or more in 1992.

Arrests
Three points need to be made with respect to arrests. First, attempts were made to record information about all police arrests for juveniles in the areas. However, it is very important to note that arrests followed by release without charge were not counted in this study. Wherever arrests are referred to in the text, it should be assumed that these are arrests that were proceeded with by the police to the point at least of charge or caution. A proportion will subsequently have been dropped after charge.

Second, in both the London areas and the Midlands county, the police were reasonably confident that they would have records on their files both of arrests that occurred on their area, and also arrests involving these juveniles *outside* the area. Inevitably, however, this is likely to be an underestimate of arrests committed outside the area because of the difficulties inherent in the transfer and updating of such information between the different forces. In both areas, informal discussions with police officers who dealt on a daily basis with juvenile arrests suggested there may have been a small group of children who were arrested three times in the year, but where none of the arrests resulted in charges, or where some of the arrests took place on another police force area, and where it therefore appeared from the local records that they had not been arrested three times. Hence, the numbers of children arrested three times or more may be an slight underestimate.

Finally, as will be visible in the body of the report, there is an imprecise match between the number of arrests per person recorded in the individual police stations' daily lists of arrestees, and the numbers of arrests per person that were subsequently found recorded in the main police files. This results in a significant minority of the sample appearing to have fewer than three arrests to their name in 1992, when information is taken from the main police files. The discrepancy arose because the main files were incomplete, but we are confident that every member of the sample was actually arrested and charged or cautioned at least three times. Information about each arrest was, however, not always placed in central records.

Offences

For the purposes of this report, it is particularly important to keep in mind the distinction between 'known' and 'alleged' offending. The latter include those cases in which offenders were arrested and charged but where charges were subsequently dropped or dismissed by the court, discontinued by the Crown Prosecution Service (CPS), still pending court, or where the offenders were found not guilty. By contrast, 'known' offending includes only those cases in which a conviction or caution was the result. Cautions are included with convictions as they require an admission of guilt. Some analyses will include only known offences, some both known and alleged, depending on the nature of the question. As Chapter 5 will show, data were collected on 3811 *known or alleged* offences committed by these 531 offenders, of which 2885 were 'known'. In addition to these two categories of known and alleged offending, another type of offence exists, namely those 'taken into consideration' (TIC'd) by a court when making sentencing decisions. Strictly speaking these offences are known to have been committed by the young person but in practice information about their number and type and date is sketchy. Throughout this report, therefore, 'known' offending does not include TICs unless otherwise stated.

Notes

1. The focus of the study was on juvenile offending in 1992. The Criminal Justice Act did not come into force until 1 October of that year, and therefore records included 17 year-olds for only the final three months. It was logical, therefore, to focus on 10 to 16 year-olds and exclude 17 year-olds.

2. It was not unusual for offenders to be known by two names, either to confuse the police or because their family formations had changed several times. They also cited a variety of dates of birth on arrest. Originally all names and dates of birth were recorded; we spent some time afterwards determining which was the correct date by cross-checking with information from other agencies and sources.

3 The Sample of Young Reoffenders

Over 500 young people were identified in the two study areas who had been arrested at least three times in 1992. This chapter describes their characteristics and discusses the representativeness of the interviewed sample.

Number of young people arrested three times

Table 3.1 below summarises the number of juveniles aged between 10 and 16 on 1 January 1992, who were arrested three times or more in 1992 (up to and including 31 December), according to daily police lists of young people arrested in their areas. In the London Boroughs 1 and 2, 44 and 67 juveniles respectively met the criterion. In the Midlands county, 420 juveniles were listed as having been arrested three times or more.

Table 3.1   Number of juveniles aged 10-16, arrested three times or more in 1992, by area

Area	Boys		Girls		Total
	n	(%)	n	(%)	n
London Borough 1	41	(93.2)	3	(6.8)	44
London Borough 2	65	(97.0)	2	(3.0)	67
Midlands County	353	(84.0)	67	(16.0)	420
Total	459	(86.4)	72	(13.6)	531

The two noticeable things about Table 3.1 are the much larger numbers of juveniles who met the criterion in the Midlands county, and the difference in the sex distributions between the three areas. The larger number of juveniles in the Midlands county is at least partly explained by the relative number of young people in the area, which is higher in the Midlands than either of the London boroughs. The preliminary 1991 census data available at the time of writing only allows approximate calculations to be done on the population figures for the age groups. Calculating the rate of young reoffenders per head of child population in each area gives ratios of 1:350 for London Borough 1, 1:250 for London Borough 2 and 1:200 for the Midlands county. Obviously, these rates are a rough and ready estimate, but they indicate that once the population base is taken into account, the differences between the areas lessen. However, it still remained the case that there were relatively more reoffenders per head of child population in the Midlands than in the London areas. There are a number of possible explanations for this, the most likely of which would be differences in policing practice with juveniles.

The difference in the proportions of girls in the three areas is less easy to explain. The proportion of girls in the Midlands sample was substantially larger than the proportion in the London sample (girls comprised 16 per cent of the sample in the Midlands compared to 5 per cent of the London sample). There are several possible explanations, and each would require more investigation. Once again, the first and most likely explanation is that there was a difference in the way that the respective police forces processed girls who are caught offending. It may be simply that the Midlands force were more likely to bring a charge than the Metropolitan police. The second possibility is that there was a difference in the offending patterns of girls in the Midlands, when compared to the offending of girls in London, though this is unlikely. Thus, for example, it is possible that girls in the Midlands were more likely to be involved in *frequent* offending in the Midlands. A third possibility is that girls were less likely to be caught in London.

From this point onwards, the two London boroughs will usually be treated together as a single 'London' group.

Ethnicity

In both areas, London and the Midlands county, the police were required to record ethnicity according to a relatively simplified categorisation. The most common code used by the police was 'WE' (White European). The other codes included 'AC' (Afro-Caribbean), 'DE' (Dark European), 'AS' (Indian/Indian/Pakistani), 'C' (Chinese/Japanese), 'DO' (Half-caste or 'Doubtful') and 'UN' (Unknown).

There were substantial area differences in whether or not it was usually possible to find a police ethnicity rating in the individual's police files. In addition, where the police had made a rating, in the London areas it was frequently a rating of unknown or doubtful. For half of the files in London Borough 1, the child's ethnicity was unknown. This was the case for 16 per cent of the files in London Borough 2 and 5 per cent of the files in the

Midlands. Because of the substantial amount of missing information, it is not possible to draw any firm conclusions about the distribution of offenders between ethnic groups in the two areas. Nor is it possible to make any useful comparisons between the police and interviewers' assessments of ethnic group, because only a few cases had information from both sources.

Age

As explained above, to be included in the study all young offenders had to have been aged 10 years or over, and under 17 years, on 1 January 1992. There were several children aged 17 or over but whose details were still in the juvenile lists but, as explained on page 34, footnote 1, these were excluded from the study. Table 3.2 shows the distribution of the children across the age range 10 to 16 (on 1 January 1992), demonstrating that taking the cut-off of three arrests or more in one year produced a group where the most frequent ages were 15 and 14, with approximately equal numbers of 13 and 16 year-olds and fewer 10-12 year-olds.

Table 3.2   Sample age distribution

Age on 1 January 1992	Number of reoffenders	(Per cent)
10	14	(2.6)
11	25	(4.7)
12	53	(10.0)
13	88	(16.6)
14	111	(20.9)
15	153	(28.8)
16	87	(16.4)
Total	531	(100.0)

Figure 3.1 summarises the number of offences committed in 1992 by each different year group in the sample. The offences in this figure are all known offences only, that is, offences that resulted in a caution or a conviction. A full discussion of offences and offending rates will be given below, but for the time being it is important to note that there was only a slight tendency for the older children to commit more offences in the year. This suggests that although there were fewer 10, 11 and 12 year-olds than

Figure 3.1   Relationship between age and offence rates

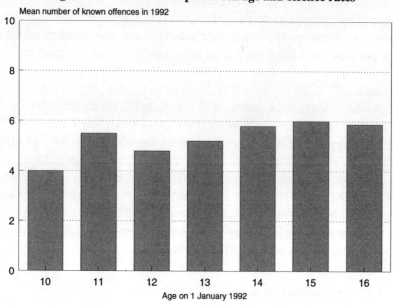

Mean number of known offences in 1992

Age on 1 January 1992

15 year-olds in the sample, among those who had crossed the 3+ arrests threshold the younger children had been cautioned or convicted as often as the 15 year-olds.

Given that the age when known offending is most frequent is 18 for boys and 15 for girls, offending might have been expected to increase with age within this sample, so that, amongst those with three or more arrests, the older children would have the most offences. In fact, there is only a slight increase of this kind which suggests that among those offending at a fairly high rate age ceases to be related to offending.

Current education and work circumstances

Data were available on the current living circumstances of the 74 reoffenders who were interviewed. These offenders were asked about their current situation and employment status. The majority of the interviewees had left school (Figure 3.2). Approximately a third were still attending or were expceted to return after the summer break. This third were almost exclusively boys, which will partly be a function of the fact that the boys tended to be younger than the girls.

Of those who were 16 or over, all had left school. In addition, eight children who were under 16 also reported having left school permanently. Several of these school leavers had plans to attend college later in the year, but the majority were otherwise engaged, as Table 3.3 summarises.

Figure 3.2   Current school situation

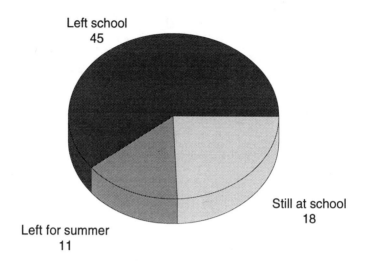

Left school
45

Still at school
18

Left for summer
11

Most of these young people reported that they were either unemployed (34 per cent) or doing something other than working, studying, training or in unemployment (16 per cent). Most of this last group were, in effect, doing nothing. Only two reoffenders were on a training scheme at the time of the interview, and one of these was on a scheme for 'joy-riders'. Thus, a significant proportion of these young people were falling through the various state systems that might have provided them with training or employment of some kind. For the purposes of this table, children who were working as well as waiting for school to resume again after the summer break will have been rated as working.

All interviewees were asked whether or not they had children. One of the boys and one of the girls was a parent, and three girls were currently pregnant. In addition, two boys' partners were expecting a child. In one case, a young woman of 17 had a three year-old child, and was pregnant again at the time of the interview. As there were only eight girls, who were aged approximately 16, this is a high proportion to have borne or be bearing children. Respondents were not asked about pregnancies that had been terminated, but it is likely that the actual number of pregnancies in this group was more than those resulting in birth, given that this would be the case in most other samples of childbearing women. Although the sample is small, the rate of teenage pregnancies was very high in comparison to national figures; in Britain, the total number of teenagers becoming pregnant each year is approximately 100,000 only, and not all will go to term (Hudson and Ineichen, 1991).

Table 3.3   Current living circumstances

	Number of reoffenders	(Per cent)
School	22	(29.7)
Waiting for college/FE	6	(8.1)
Studying full-time, other than school	0	(0.0)
Working full-time	4	(5.4)
Working part-time	1	(1.4)
Training scheme	2	(3.7)
Unemployed	25	(33.8)
Something else, non-employed	12	(16.2)
Total	74	(100.0)

The occupational status of their fathers and mothers or other male and female heads of the household are shown in Figure 3.3. In a large proportion of cases, the interviewees reported that their mothers (or female heads of household) and fathers (or male heads of household) were either not working or unemployed (62 per cent of mothers and 42 per cent of fathers). This must have contributed to what one interviewer recorded as 'an air of extreme poverty' at an interviewee's house. Six mothers and six fathers were involved in non-manual work; the remainder were in skilled or unskilled manual work. Since this question was asked in order to assess household social class, interviewees may have been describing the working status of their grandmother, sister, or father's partner, the most frequent substitutes for mother as head of household, and similarly they may have been describing grandfathers or brothers or mother's partners instead of fathers.

Sample representativeness
How representative is the interviewed sample of the full group of offenders arrested three times or more? The interviewed sample was compared with the full group of 531 offenders, comparing them on sex, age on 1 January 1992, and number of known and alleged offences. A series of analyses suggested, as expected, that there was a slight trend for interviewees to be a month or two younger, to have slightly fewer arrests, and fewer offences. However, as Table 3.4 shows, none of these differences between those

Figure 3.3   Occupational status of heads of household

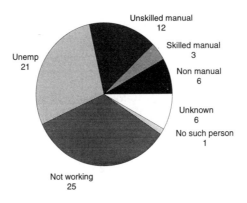

Father or male head of household

Mother or female head of household

interviewed and those not interviewed was large, and none was statistically significant. Table 3.4 also shows that the interviewed sample contained 11 per cent girls, compared to 14 per cent girls in the full group of 531 on whom police data were available. Again, this difference is not significant.

Despite the relatively low response rate, the interviewed sample does not appear to be significantly different from the complete pool of young reoffenders who were arrested three times or more in 1992, at least in terms of the variables on which they were compared: sex, age, arrest rates and official offending. However, although the intention had been to interview a representative group of the reoffenders, the interviewing had been

Table 3.4   Representativeness of interviewed sample: interviewees and full sample compared on sex, age, known and alleged offences

Comparison variable	Offenders not interviewed (total n 457)		Offenders interviewed (total n 74)		Probability[2]
	Mean	(SD)[1]	Mean	(SD)	
Age in years [A] in 1.1.92	14.5	(1.5)	14.4	(1.4)	p>.10
Total arrests 1992 [B]	4.6	(3.2)	4.5	(2.7)	p>.10
Total known and alleged offences 1992 [C]	7.5	(6.7)	7.1	(4.4)	p>.10
Total known offences 1992 [D*]	5.7	(5.9)	5.0	(4.4)	p>.10
Percentage male	86		89		p>.10

Notes
SD = Standard Deviation
A. Numbers = 456/74 B. Numbers = 438/74 C. Numbers = 436/74 D. Numbers = 439/74
*   Offences ending in caution or court prosecution only

targeted at the most frequent offenders as these were anticipated to be the most difficult to see (see p.29). Comparisons of those not chosen for interview, those chosen but not seen, and those seen, suggest that those chosen but not seen were more frequent offenders than the others[3].

Those who were not interviewed were those who were harder to contact, for example, because they often moved house, or were usually out, or nobody knew where they were. Anecdotal information was gathered from families and social workers about the children who were not interviewed. Not surprisingly, it was our impression that the children we had most difficulty interviewing were those leading the most chaotic and disturbed personal lives. Thus, for example, we had particular problems with those who were, by their family's admission, beyond the care and control of the family and also beyond the control of the local authority. Two examples illustrate these types of case. In one case, the child was not with the family and had been at a children's home approximately a month prior to our contact. However, at the children's home he had been a persistent absconder and had been missing for approximately five weeks. Even had he been present, the staff were of the opinion that he would be very unlikely to agree to talk to us. A second juvenile had also been at a children's home some

Table 3.5   Mean age of interviewed sample on 1 July 1993

	Mean age	(SD)	Cases
Total sample interviewed	15.9	(1.2)	74
Girls	16.2	(1.6)	8
Boys	15.8	(1.3)	66

SD = Standard Deviation

months previously, but had disappeared and neither the family nor the home knew where he was permanently based. We spoke to the children's home on a Monday, and he had surfaced over the weekend, spent Saturday night at the home as an emergency admission, and had then left on Sunday. The residential workers reported that the boy, who was now 13, had been in a local authority secure unit for a period when he was 12, and although he was still only small, he was out of everybody's control.

Children were interviewed who also reported equally chaotic lives, and who were in and out of different types of accommodation throughout their childhoods. Interviews were achieved in a variety of different settings including children's homes, young offenders institutions, and family homes. However, this sample may underrepresent those towards the top of the scale of lifestyle disruption, as they were the harest to see.

As described in Chapter 2, in London all reoffenders identified from the files were sought for interview, whereas in the Midlands, 140 of the 420 were selected for interview. Response rates were virtually identical in the two areas, being 27 per cent in London and 26 per cent in the Midlands.

Approximately a year had passed between the period covered by the collection of official records and the interviewing of subjects, and Table 3.5 shows the mean ages for the interviewed sample on 1 July 1993, which was in the middle of the interviewing period.

The girls who were interviewed tended to be a few months older than the boys, who were just under 16 years old during the interviewing period.

Summary
Within two geographical areas, consisting of one Midlands county and two London boroughs combined, 531 young people were arrested and charged by the police three times or more in 1992. Police data were collected on all 531 offenders and, in addition, 74 were interviewed. Of those 531 offenders for whom data were available, 14 per cent were girls. The

proportion of girls was twice as high among the Midlands as among the London offenders. Information about ethnic group was incomplete. Age was not significantly related to rates of offending among these reoffenders, although it is among the general population.

The majority of the interviewed sample reported that they had left school and were currently not doing anything structured with their time. Few were on employment or training schemes. Rates of childbirth for the girls seemed very high, but the numbers were too small to be conclusive. Approximately half of the children lived in households where the heads were not working or unemployed, and this reinforced the general picture of disadvantage that appeared to characterise the lives of these young reoffenders.

Comparisons of age, arrests and offending rates suggested that the interviewed sample were not significantly different from the full group of 531 reoffenders, but interviewing was targeted at the most frequent, and it was these who were the most difficult to see. However, anecdotal information indicated that some of the children who were not interviewed were leading very chaotic personal lives.

Notes

1. The standard deviation (SD) is a statistical method of assessing the dispersion or spread of the scores of a group as a whole. The higher the SD, the wider the spread of the scores of the individual members of the group. If the scores are normally distributed (with most responses near the mean, and equal spread each side of the mean), approximately half of the scores will always fall within one SD from the mean. Thus, if the mean is 5, and the standard deviation is 1.5, half of the scores will fall between 3.5 and 6.5.

2. In order to test whether the variations between the offenders who were interviewed and those who were not interviewed were significant, a series of statistical tests was conducted. This final column of the table presents the probability of the differences between the groups occurring by chance. In this case, the probability in every case is more than 10 per cent that the differences only reflect chance differences, not real differences in scores. The usual rule for assuming that differences between groups are statistically significant is that the probability has to be 5 per cent or less (.05).

3. A three-way comparison between those not chosen for interview, those chosen but not interviewed, and those interviewed, suggested that the interviewed group fell between the other two groups, with the least frequent offenders being those not chosen, and the most being those not seen. The differences between those chosen but not interviewed and those successfully interviewed were not statistically significant for age or sex, but were for arrest and offending rates. The interviewed group had, on average, two fewer arrests a year, two fewer alleged offences and two fewer known offences.

Part II

Young Reoffenders and the
Criminal Justice System

4 Patterns of Arrest

One of the two main aims of this project was fact-finding. Basic information is lacking about the backgrounds, patterns of arrest, official convictions and offence types of young people who *have been arrested repeatedly.* The four chapters in this part of the report will look at the nature of the police contact for this group of 531 young people arrested three times or more in one year, and will put together information from several sources describing their backgrounds, educational experiences, and other aspects of their lives. Part III will examine the concept of persistence, and analyse the consequences of defining it in various ways.

This first chapter of Part II describes the arrest patterns of the reoffenders as a whole. Police records provide information about all arrests but not about most other contacts with reoffenders. Of course, several of the families were well known to the police, and there were a number of ways in which the young people may have made contact with the police apart from specific arrests. For example, they may have been involved in questioning in connection with other offences for which they were not charged; they may have been involved in some cases as victims and witnesses; and they may have been present when relatives or friends were stopped or arrested by the police. However, this chapter concentrates on arrests as described by police records and by reoffenders' own accounts.

Arrest patterns

Table 4.1, which is based on files at police headquarters, shows the number of arrests in 1992 for the sample of 531 reoffenders. The first thing to notice is that there are 85 young people who, according to the files at police headquarters, do not appear to have been arrested three times or more. The most likely explanation is that the files at police headquarters are an incomplete record (see Chapter 3). Young offenders were counted as reoffenders (three or more arrests in 1992) on the basis of information kept at individual police stations. The police files centralised at headquarters consisted of information gathered from individual police stations. In the process of gathering and summarising this information, it appears that some of it was lost or disregarded. Since other information exists from individual

Table 4.1 **Total number of 1992 arrests for each young reoffender as recorded in their files at police headquarters**

Number of arrests in 1992	Number of reoffenders	(Per cent)
0	7	(1.3)
1	21	(4.2)
2	57	(11.2)
3	149	(28.3)
4	96	(19.2)
5	62	(12.4)
6	35	(6.8)
7	21	(4.2)
8	17	(3.2)
9	12	(2.3)
10	9	(1.7)
11	5	(1.1)
12	3	(0.6)
13	5	(1.1)
14	1	(0.2)
15	4	(0.8)
16	0	(0.0)
17	1	(0.2)
18	3	(0.4)
19	2	(0.4)
20	0	(0.0)
21	1	(0.2)
22	0	(0.0)
23	1	(0.2)
Total	512	(100.0)

stations that these 85 young people were arrested three times or more in 1992, they are kept in all subsequent analyses; but since these are based on the information kept at headquarters, they underestimate arrests and therefore offences.

In 19 cases information about the dates of the arrests was missing. In these cases it is not possible to count the exact number of arrests in 1992, although it is believed that these amounted to at least three. Offences can usually be counted, but where dates are missing it is not always clear whether several offences sprang from a single arrest. Where dates were missing, there is therefore a slight tendency for the number of arrests to be overstated.

From Table 4.1 it appears that the majority of these young reoffenders had been arrested three, four or five times in 1992. If it is assumed that those for whom none, one and two arrests were recorded in their police files had actually been arrested three times, then about three quarters of the sample had been arrested three, four or five times[1]. Approximately one fifth had been arrested between six and 10 times, while only 5 per cent had been arrested more than 10 times in the year. The highest number of recorded arrests for one individual in the year was 23.

Self-report of first arrest

Due to constraints of time and resources, it was not possible to record the first arrest of the whole sample from their individual files. In fact, in a proportion of cases, the record of the first arrest will have been wiped from the record due to the expiry period allowed by the Rehabilitation of Offenders Act 1974. In several cases, children will have been arrested when they were too young to have a file or a criminal record number assigned to them, so there will be no official record of this arrest.

For these reasons, the reoffenders were asked if they had ever been arrested and how old they were on the first occasion. All 74 respondents confirmed that they had been arrested. Half of them said that they had first

Table 4.2   Interviewees' reports of outcome of first arrest

	Number	(Per cent)
Nothing	11	(14.9)
Informal caution	6	(8.1)
Formal caution	51	(68.9)
Other	4	(5.4)
Couldn't remember	2	(2.7)
Total	74	(100.0)

Figure 4.1   Interviewees' reports of age at first arrest

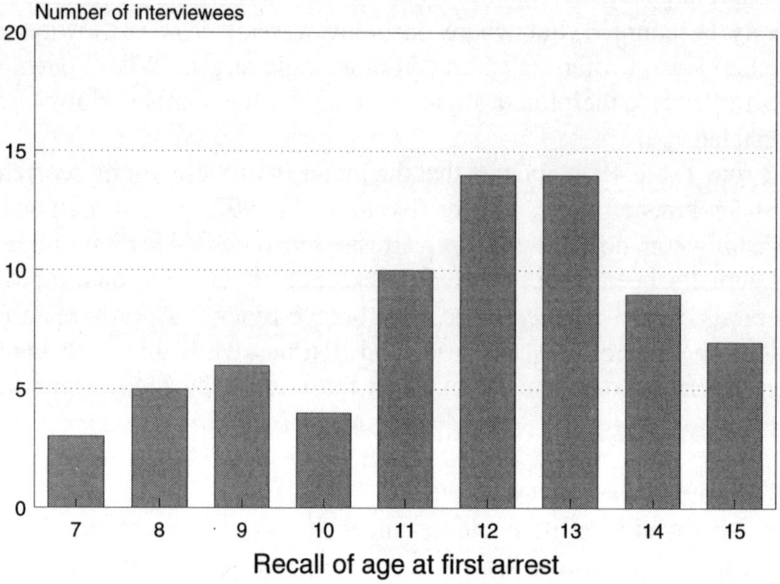

Number of interviewees

Recall of age at first arrest

2 missing cases

been arrested by the time they were 12 (Figure 4.1). The peak ages at first arrest were 12 and 13.

Two-thirds of respondents believed that they received a formal caution following their first arrest, whereas 15 per cent believed there was no outcome (Table 4.2).

Summary

This section illustrates some of the difficulties of drawing conclusions from official data that are recorded in several different places and then collected together centrally. Information from one source may not match information from another place, and the more reorganisation of information there is, the more likely it is that official information will become an underestimate of the 'real' figures, as data are probably lost at each stage. When police headquarters files were analysed for this sample of children who, according to police stations, had been arrested three times or more in 1992, the central files did not always contain details of three arrests. The police headquarters files on these young reoffenders showed that they were most usually arrested in 1992 on three, four or five occasions. A very small proportion had been arrested more than ten times, and the highest number of arrests in the year was 23.

This chapter also highlights some of the difficulties of relying on self-report assessments in research of this type (see Tarling, 1993, Chapter 1, for a fuller discussion). All that can be reported are the subjects' accounts of what happened to them, and it is not possible accurately to discover exactly what it is they mean by, for example, an arrest, without spending much more time talking to them.

Notes

1. However, the under-recording of arrests in the police files is likely to be reflected across the whole range, so that even some of the higher numbers of arrests will still represent an underestimate for those offenders.

5 Patterns of Offending

This chapter describes offending patterns among reoffenders throughout 1992, by analysing both police records and reoffenders' reports. The data drawn from police records understate the *number of offences actually processed*, for the reasons discussed in the previous chapter. Of course, official records of offenders understate the *actual level of offending* by a much wider margin, because only about one quarter of recorded offences are cleared up by the police. In order to provide descriptive information about the offending of the sample of reoffenders, this chapter reports figures from official records and from the offenders' own accounts.

Number and characteristics of offences
Charges withdrawn, cases dismissed, verdicts of 'not guilty',
cases pending
There was a combination of known and alleged offending recorded in the police files.

Table 5.1 shows that of all the 1992 offences recorded against the names of these reoffenders in police files, 67 per cent had resulted in a conviction and sentence, whereas 11 per cent had resulted in an admission of guilt and a caution. These 77 per cent are the 'known offences' recorded. The remaining 23 per cent are merely 'alleged offences'; they were pending, dismissed, discontinued, withdrawn, or resulted in a verdict of 'not guilty'[1].

Distribution of known offences
Figure 5.1 gives the number of known offences per reoffender. The mean number of offences per reoffender was 5.6, and the range was from 1 to 50. Once again, the number of offences is understated because the records are incomplete. Fourteen per cent of reoffenders had between zero and two known offences recorded in 1992, although they had been arrested at least three times in that year. As well as being the result of missing some information, this is partly because a proportion of arrests led to no caution or conviction. Very few of these reoffenders had more than 20 offences in the year; only two had more than 40.

Table 5.1   Outcome of 1992 offences recorded in police files

Disposal	Numbers	(Per cent)
No police action taken*	169	(4.2)
Caution**	423	(10.7)
Pending*	237	(6.6)
Discontinued*	72	(2.0)
Dismissed*	176	(5.9)
Withdrawn*	128	(3.6)
Not guilty (at court)*	23	(0.7)
Sentenced (at court)**	2,462	(67.3)
Total	3,690	(101.0)

Offences with no outcome recorded = 121

*   Alleged offences

**   Known offences

Figure 5.1   Total number of known offences in 1992 per reoffender

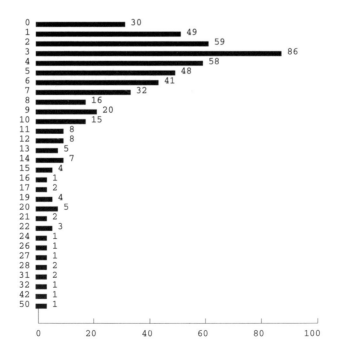

Offence number by area

Tables 5.2 and 5.3 show the average number of offences by area. The first of this pair of tables includes all *known or alleged* offences (3,811 offences), the second includes only the *known* offences that resulted in a caution or conviction (2,885 offences). From the means for the areas, it is possible to see that more offences were dropped at an earlier stage in the London boroughs than was the case in the Midlands. Thus, the mean number of offences per individual offender for the Midlands county dropped from 7.7 alleged and known offences to 6.1 known offences, whereas in the London borough it dropped from 6.4 to 4.1. There was a statistically significant[2] difference between the areas in the mean number of known offences per reoffender (higher in the Midlands county) but not in the mean number of total alleged *and* known offences per reoffender.

Table 5.2   Mean offence numbers by area: all alleged and known 1992 offences

	Mean number of offences	(SD)	Cases
London	6.4	(4.3)	111
Midlands	7.7	(6.9)	402

F = 3.4, df 1,411, p.>05 (not significant)[3]
SD = Standard Deviation
Individuals where total could not be calculated due to some missing information = 18

Table 5.3   Mean offence numbers by area: known offending only

	Mean number of offences	(SD)	Cases
London	4.1	(3.9)	111
Midlands	6.1	(6.1)	402

F=10.6, df 1,511, p.05[3]
SD = Standard Deviation
Individuals where total could not be calculated due to some missing information = 18

From this point onward, the analysis concentrates for the most part on the known offences in 1992 recorded against this sample of young people who had been arrested three or more times in the course of that year.

Offence types, overall and by area

These reoffenders committed a wide range of offences. Table 5.4 below gives an overall summary of all the offences by type, for a total of 2,885 offences known to have been committed by these reoffenders in 1992. This list, whilst extensive, is itself a shortened version of the full list of categories that were used to code the police data. These are shown in Appendix 4.

Table 5.4   Type and numbers of known offences

Offence types	Numbers	(Per cent)
Road traffic offence	411	(14.2)
Burglary - other & unspecified	374	(13.1)
Car theft	304	(10.6)
Criminal damage (including arson)	237	(8.2)
Theft from shop	222	(7.7)
Theft unspecified	205	(7.1)
Actual bodily harm	193	(6.7)
Bail, procedural	129	(4.5)
Handling stolen goods	123	(4.3)
Theft from car	100	(3.5)
Theft of cycle	100	(3.5)
Public order	92	(3.2)
Burglary - residential	83	(2.9)
Robbery	63	(2.2)
Going equipped to steal	55	(1.9)
Possession of a weapon	37	(1.3)
Aggravated car theft	32	(1.1)
Drugs offences	33	(1.1)
Other	27	(0.9)
Prostitution	19	(0.7)
Grievous bodily harm	12	(0.4)
Sexual	9	(0.3)
Total offences*	2,860	(100.0)

Offences missing a type coding = 25
* Excluding not guilty, dismissed, withdrawn, pending and no further action.

Table 5.5   Area differences in offence types and numbers

Offence type	London n	London (%)	Midlands n	Midlands (%)	Overall (%)
Road traffic offence	94	(20.8)	317	(13.2)	(14.4)
Burglary - other and unspecified	55	(12.2)	319	(13.2)	(13.1)
Car theft	25	(5.5)	279	(11.6)	(10.6)
Criminal damage (including arson)	20	(4.4)	217	(9.0)	(8.3)
Theft from shop	48	(10.6)	174	(7.2)	(7.8)
Theft unspecified	28	(6.2)	177	(7.4)	(7.2)
Actual bodily harm	18	(4.0)	175	(7.3)	(6.7)
Bail, procedural	5	(1.1)	124	(5.1)	(4.5)
Handling stolen goods	23	(5.1)	100	(4.2)	(4.3)
Theft from car	21	(4.6)	79	(3.3)	(3.5)
Theft of cycle	9	(2.0)	91	(3.8)	(3.5)
Public order	24	(5.3)	68	(2.8)	(3.2)
Burglary - residential	10	(2.2)	73	(3.0)	(2.9)
Robbery	21	(4.6)	42	(1.7)	(2.2)
Going equipped	7	(1.5)	48	(2.0)	(1.9)
Possession of weapon	15	(3.3)	22	(0.9)	(1.3)
Drugs offences	15	(3.3)	18	(0.7)	(1.2)
Aggravated car theft	2	(0.4)	30	(1.2)	(1.1)
Other	8	(1.8)	19	(0.8)	(0.9)
Prostitution	0	(0.0)	19	(0.8)	(0.7)
Grievous bodily harm	3	(0.7)	9	(0.4)	(0.4)
Sexual	1	(0.2)	8	(0.3)	(0.3)
	452	(100.0)	2,408	(100.0)	(100.0)

Total offences = 2,885, excluding not guilty, dismissed, withdrawn, pending, no further action.
Total missing type coding = 25

The types of offence committed by these young reoffenders were broadly similar to those committed by juveniles in general. (For comparative figures, see *Criminal Statistics*, any year. For self-report data on adolescents, see Farrington, 1979; Tarling, 1993.) Road traffic offences, non-residential burglary, car theft, and criminal damage were amongst the most common offences. Other categories of theft were also fairly common. Reflecting the general trend for most juvenile offending to be non-violent, actual bodily harm accounted for less than 7 per cent of offences committed by these reoffenders, grievous bodily harm for 0.4 per cent.

Offences for which young reoffenders were cautioned or convicted differed slightly between London and the Midlands (see Table 5.5). In the London areas, the four most common offence types were non-residential (or unspecified) burglary, road traffic offences, theft from shop, and unspecified theft, in that order. In the Midlands, the four most common offence types were non-residential burglary, road traffic offences, car theft and criminal damage, in that order. In London, the two rarest offence types were prostitution and sexual offences. In the Midlands, the two rarest types were sexual offences and grievous bodily harm. These area differences – which in any case are not large – may reflect differences in policing priorities or prosecution practice rather than different patterns of offending. In addition, area differences might have been expected given the fact that the Midlands county covered rural areas as well as cities.

Offences taken into consideration

The recording of offences that were taken into consideration (TIC'd) at court is incomplete. The London files did not contain systematic – or indeed any – information about offences that were TIC'd. The information in the Midlands files was frequently at odds with that on the computer printout of criminal records, even when the court date matched. Where TICs were indicated on the court printout but not in the police files, there were no dates of offences nor offence types given. Even where the police files suggested TICs, it was not always possible to date and type them. It is our impression that TICs cannot be usefully analysed from the police files. Potentially, it would be possible to assess TICs from the full court records, where it is more likely that dates and types are more fully recorded, but court records were not always available on the files for these reoffenders.

Against that background, Table 5.6 shows the total distribution of TICs for the Midlands reoffenders. From this it is clear that when TICs are put before a court, they tend to be substantial in number. Of the 31 per cent of Midlands reoffenders with any TICs (and this will be a sum of all received across the whole year) half had 10 or more, and a quarter 17 or more. Given that the average number of known offences for the Midlands was six, these figures are relatively high. If the mean known offences for the Midlands sample is recalculated to include TICs, the figure rises from six to ten

Table 5.6   **Total number of offences taken into consideration for each reoffenders in the Midlands county in 1992**

Number of TICs in 1992	Number of juveniles	(Per cent)
0	275	(68.9)
1	18	(4.5)
2	10	(2.5)
3	6	(1.5)
4	9	(2.3)
5	7	(1.8)
6	4	(1.1)
7	9	(2.3)
8	5	(1.3)
9	3	(0.8)
10	3	(0.8)
11	2	(0.5)
12	6	(1.5)
13	1	(0.3)
14	2	(0.5)
15	2	(0.5)
16	2	(0.5)
17	2	(0.5)
18	0	(0.0)
19	1	(0.2)
20	1	(0.2)
21-50	23	(6.0)
51-100	7	(1.8)
100+	1	(0.3)
Total	399	(100.0)

Missing cases = 21

offences per reoffender. However, given the fact that the data on TICs were only available for the Midlands sample, that only a third of them had TICs, and within that third the number of TICs ranged from 1 to 109, inclusion of TICs into the statistics is likely to make the figures less meaningful. Where TICs were given offence types, the majority were for offences of burglary, car theft, unspecified and attempted theft and criminal damage.

Offending according to the reoffender's characteristics
Sex and offending

Girls accounted for 16 per cent of the sample of reoffenders in the Midlands, compared with 5 per cent in London. However, among girls above the threshold of three arrests in 1992, and therefore included in the sample, the mean number of known offences was about the same as for the boys, both overall, and in each of the two areas (Table 5.7). The probability that a girl will become a reoffender is much lower than that for a boy, but among those who cross the threshold, the rate of offending is about the same for the sexes. This suggests a strong polarisation between non-offending and reoffending girls.

Table 5.7   Frequency of known offending by sex

	Average known offences 1992	(SD)	n
Girls	5.5	(3.8)	70
Boys	5.7	(5.9)	443
All	5.6	(5.7)	513

F = .06, df 1,511, p>.05 (not significant)
Individuals where total could not be calculated due to some missing information = 18

Were the girls committing different types of offences from the boys? In order to investigate this question, the offence types were grouped into five categories: burglary, car theft, other theft, violent offences, including actual bodily harm (ABH), and other. The analysis considered whether each offender had or had not committed each of the five types of offence in 1992. Nearly twice as many of the girls as the boys had committed violent offences (49 per cent compared with 28 per cent). Although physical aggression is much more common among males than among females in general, this surprising finding shows that within the highly selected group of reoffenders, arrests for violent offences are more common among the females. This may reflect differences in arrest practices for violence by girls, but further research would be needed to determine any reasons for the differences. The finding that more girls than boys had committed some kind of theft (77 per cent compared with 63 per cent) was more in line with expectation. The boys were more likely to have committed a burglary (48 per cent of the boys and 29 per cent of the girls), and more likely to have

Figure 5.2   Specialisation or diversification of crime: number of different types recorded for each reoffender in 1992

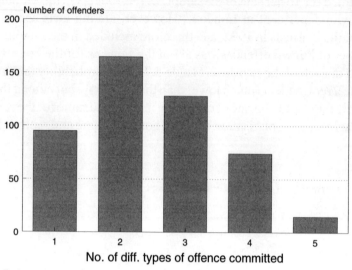

483 offenders

committed car theft of some kind (38 per cent of the boys compared to 22 per cent of the girls). The violence for which the girls had been convicted was usually actual bodily harm (rather than grievous bodily harm).

Diversity and specialisation of offending

It is frequently suggested, particularly by the media, that there are certain persistent young offenders who specialise in certain types of crime, for example, only or mainly taking cars or committing burglaries. Using the same five groups of offences defined in the section above, each offender was assigned a score from 1 to 5 depending on how many different *types* of offence he or she had committed. Although the offence groups were broad, the analysis provides a good indication of the extent to which reoffenders tended to specialise.

Figure 5.2 shows that the reoffenders rarely specialised by these criteria. Only 20 per cent of the 458 offenders for whom this exercise could be done had known offences of just one type during the 1992 period. The majority of reoffenders had scored known offences of two or three different types of offence, and a fifth had scored four or five types. These are all fairly frequent offenders. However, those with one type of offence were those who committed few offences in total, whereas those committing five different types were those with a large number of offences. Thus, those with one type of offence had committed an average of two known offences during the

**Figure 5.3   Proportion of offenders committing different types of offence
at least once**

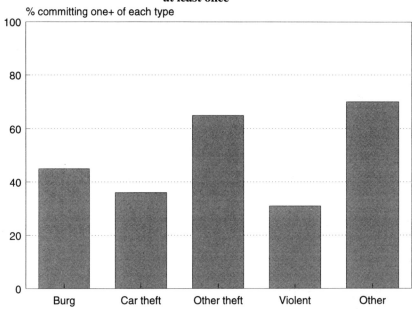

483 offenders

year; those with two types of offence had committed an average of four known offences; and those with five types had committed an average of 17 known offences. This suggested that specialisation was related to extent of offending during the year, contradicting the idea that frequent offenders specialise in certain types of crime.

Figure 5.3, which gives the proportion of offenders who had committed any given offence type, demonstrates, in a different way, that reoffenders had frequently recorded known offences of several types. This is shown by the fact that such substantial proportions had recorded known offences of each type considered in turn. These proportions were nearly half for burglary, two-thirds for other theft, one third for violent offences and car theft, and more than two-thirds for other offences. Clearly the same individuals had to be committing offences of several different types to produce this pattern of results.

Although these figures are striking, analysis of the actual number of individuals who had committed the offences suggests that they should be treated with some caution. Although it seems dramatic that one third of these young reoffenders had committed a violent crime, in fact only 151 reoffenders in three geographical areas over a whole calendar year had recorded a known offence of violence (including robbery), and many of these offences were classified as actual bodily harm, not grievous bodily harm. Although the data do not show that violence is common among the general population of juveniles, they do show that it is relatively common among this small group of reoffenders. Nevertheless, serious violence (grievous bodily harm) remains rare even among reoffenders, and is confined to a small number of them (11 in this sample). In 1992, there were no known offences of rape, murder, or manslaughter by young reoffenders in this sample.

Offending in company
Proportion of offences committed with others
Previous research has concluded that young offenders frequently offend in pairs or groups (for a review of research see Reiss and Farrington, 1991; Tarling, 1993). In such circumstances a single incident gives rise to several offences. It follows that the number of offences in some categories give an inflated impression of the number of incidents, because these offences are commonly committed by groups. Thus, car theft is not usually a solo crime, whereas possession of an offensive weapon has to be a solo offence, as two people cannot simultaneously possess the same weapon.

This study is in the unusual position of being able to assess the number of those offences where a pair or a group were charged with the offence rather than an individual. Where existing literature refers to offending 'company', it is usually based on court records that note that there were co-defendants. However, a proportion of those charged in connection with the same incident will not go on to be co-defendants, as their cases may be discontinued or withdrawn, or they may simply be processed separately. The data regarding co-offenders in the police files are, therefore, likely to be a better estimate of co-offending than court records, although police data are also likely to be an underestimate, since co-chargees are not always systematically recorded by the police, nor indeed, of course, are co-offenders always arrested. Police files do not routinely record the *presence* of others when the offender is charged; where data do exist, they record only whether others were *charged* with the offence.

Because of the difficulty of assessing where 'company' begins and ends, it was decided that certain offences could be coded only as 'solo' offences even if others were present. Thus, possession of an offensive weapon and going equipped to steal will always have been recorded as solo offences, even if others were present and charged for possession of different weapons at the same time.

Figure 5.4 shows the proportion of those offences that were clearly recorded in the police files as being committed by two or more offenders.

Figure 5.4   Proportion of offences committed with other offenders

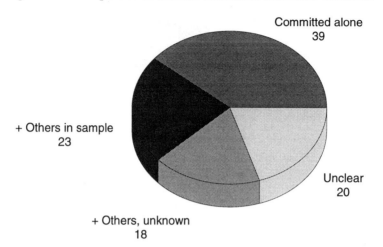

Committed alone
39

+ Others in sample
23

Unclear
20

+ Others, unknown
18

2885 'known' offences

A distinction was drawn between 'company' where that was another member of the selected sample of reoffenders who were arrested three times or more, and 'company' where the person was not in the sample. As a matter of interest, it was noticed in several cases that the 'company' was another member of the same family: a brother, parent or other relative. There was at least one case where a boy was being taken on burglaries by his father, and one where a girl was involved in prostitution with her mother. However, in these tables the distinction is not made between relatives and others.

Of those offences where it was possible to tell whether there had been a co-offender or not, just under half were committed alone.

Proportion of reoffenders offending with others

Turning this question on its head, one might ask how many offenders tend to commit offences with others. If reoffenders committed *any* of their offences with another person, they were rated '1'. If they committed *any* of their offences with others in the sample, they were rated '2'. Figure 5.5 shows that most reoffenders had committed at least one offence with other people, most frequently with other people in the area who had also been arrested three times or more.

Figure 5.5   Proportion of offenders committing any offences with others

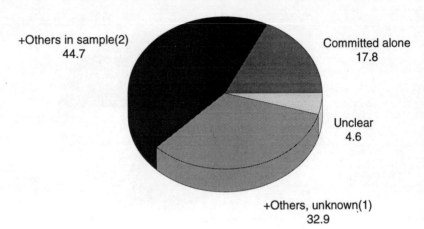

+Others in sample(2)
44.7

Committed alone
17.8

Unclear
4.6

+Others, unknown(1)
32.9

2885 'known' offences

These figures can only skim the surface of what is, potentially, an extremely interesting and productive avenue of exploration. They suggest that many of these offenders know each other, and that their offending is far from being a solitary affair. Others have suggested that the influence of others or the desire to perform in front of friends is likely to be a substantial motivating factor in offending behaviour, and these results suggest that this may well be the case.

Police action after arrest: the use of bail and custody
On arresting and charging a juvenile, the police must decide either to release the person on bail, to keep him or her overnight in police custody, or to transfer to the custody of the local authority. It was not possible to distinguish between the two types of overnight custody. Overall comparisons between bail and custody in Figure 5.6 suggest that in the majority of cases, these offenders were bailed to reappear at the police station or court. If calculations are based only on those reoffenders either bailed or kept (excluding unknowns or cautions), 64 per cent were bailed. In cases where offenders were cautioned, any other police action was not coded, so they appear on this table as a separate case, although some of them will have been bailed or kept and then cautioned at a later date. In 20

Figure 5.6   Immediate police action following arrest

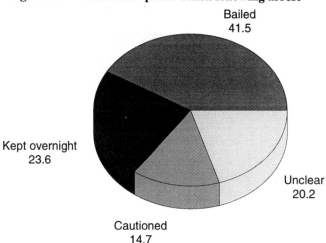

2885 'known' offences

per cent of cases, it was not possible to tell from the files whether or not the offender was bailed or kept.

Offending on bail

One of the major concerns expressed in recent months has been that large numbers of young offenders were committing offences while on bail for a previous offence. One of the aims of this study, therefore, was to collect data on the bail status of young offenders at the time they committed offences in order to establish not only the proportion of offences committed by reoffenders who are on bail but also the proportion of reoffenders committing offences while on bail.

Proportion of offences committed whilseon bail

The majority (56 per cent) of the known offences recorded in the study were committed while the offender was on bail for other offences, as is shown in Figure 5.7.

It was not possible to distinguish between bail that had been set by the police and bail set by the court. Neither was it possible to look at conditional bail, curfews, other refinements to the bail notice, or whether or not the child was on remand to the local authority at the time of the offence. In addition, as mentioned above, some offenders will have been bailed and

Figure 5.7   Bail status of offender when offence was committed

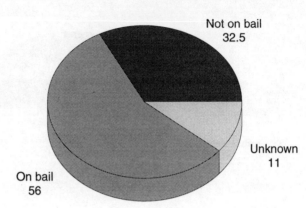

Not on bail
32.5

Unknown
11

On bail
56

2885 'known' offences

then returned to the police station for cautioning at a later date, so the number of offences committed on bail might be an underestimate. There were small area differences in the number of offences committed on bail, in that a slightly larger proportion of offences recorded in the Midlands were recorded as having occurred while the offender was on bail. However, the volume of information in the Midlands police files concerning each offence was usually larger, and it may simply have been that it was easier to confirm that this was the case with Midlands offences. The *types* of offence committed on bail were not different from offences not committed on bail.

Proportion of reoffenders committing offences on bail
If offenders committed any one of their offences (for which they were cautioned or successfully prosecuted) while they were on bail, they were recorded as having committed offences on bail. Figure 5.8 shows that approximately 60 per cent of all reoffenders for whom this information is available had committed offences while on police or court bail. This figure looks high, but findings presented below demonstrate that the time between offence and final sentence could be very long, and the majority of these children will have spent most of the year on bail.

Figure 5.8   Proportion of offenders committing any offences on bail

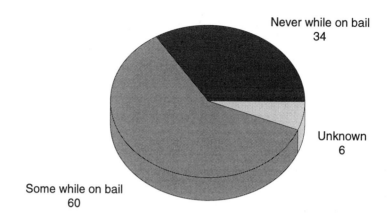

Never while on bail
34

Unknown
6

Some while on bail
60

2885 'known' offences

The value of offences

The sum of money stolen or the value of the theft or criminal damage was not systematically recorded in the police files. A value in pounds was recorded for a total of 619 offences, so the conclusions that may be drawn from the overall value of the offences committed by these reoffenders are limited. Figure 5.9 portrays the distribution of values for those 619 offences. The police are probably unlikely to record very small values anyway, and so the sums that were recorded appeared to be fairly substantial. The figure suggests that the largest proportion of offences were valued at between £10 and £100. Seventy-three offences were valued at over £1,000, and, in fact, four of these were valued at over £20,000. For most of these larger sums, the offence will have involved substantial damage to very expensive cars. In a few cases, it involved taking expensive items such as fax machines and computers from shops or offices.

Self-reported offending

It has already been suggested that the police figures accessed for this study were likely to be an underestimate of 'official' offending amongst this group. Also, crime surveys demonstrate (Hough and Mayhew, 1985; Mayhew et al, 1989) that officially-recorded crime substantially underestimates actual crime. As was suggested in Chapter 1, self-reported

Figure 5.9   Value of offences: amount theft or damage where value is known

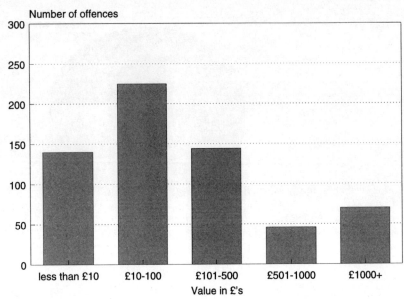

619 offences only

offending also understates actual levels of offending, especially for serious crimes (Tarling, 1993). Since bias is likely, and since little is known about the self-reports of juveniles who offend fairly frequently, these data should be treated with some caution.

Range and frequency of self-reported offending in the month prior to interview

Self-reported offending was assessed using the self-report check list given to interviewees to complete themselves during the interview (see Chapter 2). Confidentiality was stressed, and the list was not scored until the interviewer had returned to the research office. For those with reading problems, the list was read aloud, but efforts were made to ensure that their responses were not observed.

Interviewees made use of all the categories listed, and therefore reported a wide variety of offences. They were asked to indicate whether or not they had *ever* committed the acts and to write the total number of times that they had committed the act in the *last month*.

The list of self-reported offences in Table 5.8 was not directly comparable to the categories presented for the official police data presented in Tables 5.4 and 5.5, which would not have been entirely meaningful to respondents. The list used in the survey was broadly comparable to that

Table 5.8   Self-reported offending: ever and last month

Self-reported offences	Per cent of interviewees admitting offence ever	Number of offenders committing offence in last month	Mean frequency in last month	(SD)
Shop theft	82	53	2.3	(5.3)
Car theft	70	45	3.3	(9.0)
Fighting	70	46	2.2	(5.0)
TWOC, TDA	70	45	1.0	(2.0)
Trespassing for theft	66	42	1.0	(3.9)
Stolen goods	66	41	3.3	(6.7)
Carried weapon	65	40	5.2	(9.9)
Hurt someone	65	41	1.6	(3.0)
Criminal damage	62	40	0.9	(1.5)
18 certificate film	60	40	1.7	(4.8)
Fare evasion	57	35	3.8	(6.8)
Disqualified driving, no insurance	54	35	6.7	(12.1)
Bought drugs	55	36	10.0	(12.2)
House theft	47	30	1.4	(4.7)
Graffiti	45	32	3.2	(7.4)
Stolen money from machine	38	27	0.6	(1.8)
Disqualified driving, no licence	35	23	4.7	(8.1)
Arson	34	24	0.3	(0.7)
Sold stolen goods	31	20	0.5	(1.1)
Theft from person	22	17	0.7	(2.4)
Sold drugs	22	13	0.5	(1.4)
Threatened someone	19	15	0.8	(2.1)
Drunk driving	12	10	3.4	(9.4)

used in the current Home Office survey of self-reported offending. It included offences from the non-criminal (getting into an 18 certificate film) to the very serious. Most of the offences are self-explanatory. Both the police and the young offenders refer to car theft as 'TWOC and TDA', and the separate category of 'car theft', in this case, means stealing *from* cars. 'Stolen goods' refers either to buying or selling.

The first column of Table 5.8 presents the proportions saying they had ever committed the offences. In addition, the table also gives the mean number of times they had committed the offence in the last month (second column), if they had said that they had ever done it. Those who had not committed the offence were not included in the calculations of means.

If these are reliable reports of undetected offending, then official records of offences must be a substantial underestimate. For every offence, at least 10 per cent of these more frequent offenders said that they had committed it at some point in their lives. The list was very varied, and consisted of 23 serious and less serious offences, so combining them is difficult, but on average more frequent reoffenders reported having committed 11.5 different types of offences at some point in their offending careers.

The most common offences on the basis of self-reports were getting into 18 certificate films, stealing from shops, stealing cars and stealing from cars, handling stolen goods, carrying offensive weapons and fighting (over 60 per cent in each case). In terms of frequency in the last month (over six times), the offences said to be committed most often were disqualified driving for reasons of no insurance or no licence, carrying weapons and buying drugs. It should be noted that carrying weapons was classified separately from actually threatening people in any way, or hurting people. It is difficult to assess in terms of frequency. Generally, subjects counted the number of days on which they had carried weapons.

The most noticeable difference between the most common offences on this list and those most commonly recorded by the police is the higher profile of buying drugs on the self-report list. The police records showed that these offenders were rarely prosecuted for drugs offences; such offences were rare (1.2 per cent of all known offences). However, 55 per cent of the reoffenders said that they had bought drugs, and those who were buying drugs were doing so relatively frequently (10 times a month). As will become clear in the penultimate part of the report, drug use amongst this group was very frequent. The discrepancy between levels officially recorded and self-reported drugs offences will be partly explained by the relative infrequency of detection and prosecution.

Summary
On average, these reoffenders were arrested four times in 1992, the most frequent number of arrests being 23 in the year. Approximately 16 per cent of the offences with which they were charged in 1992 were withdrawn or otherwise dismissed. The remaining offences resulted in either a caution or a prosecution. The distribution of the offences across this group of reoffenders did not suggest a substantial group of very frequent offenders, but this issue will be returned to in Chapter 8, which considers the implications of adopting various different definitions of persistence within this sample. Reoffenders in the Midlands tended to have a larger number

of known offences than the London children. We were not able to code systematically from the police files offences taken into consideration and admitted by the offender and were not included in the analyses, except in a limited way.

Although girls were much less likely than boys to qualify as reoffenders, girls and boys who had been arrested three or more times in 1992 had been charged with similar numbers of offences. The reoffenders in the sample did not specialise in broad categories of crime. Instead, they tended to commit crimes over a range of different offence types. Many offences were committed with others. After arrest, the majority were bailed. A substantial proportion of offenders committed offences while on bail.

Official records of numbers of offences and self-reported offending differed substantially. These reoffenders admitted to having committed a wide range of offences in their lives, and to having committed a large number in the last month. Although the most common self-reported offences were not dissimilar from the most common offences highlighted in the official records of offending – being mostly theft of one sort or another or driving offences – drugs offences had a far higher profile in the self-report list than was the case in the police records.

Notes

1. The London area operated a Youth Panel, consisting of the police and representatives from agencies involved in the welfare of young people such as social services. Such panels will have had a role to play in deciding which cases to proceed with and which to drop, from both the perspective of the welfare of the child and that of the criminal justice system. The Midlands area did not operate such a panel.

2. As described in Note 1 of Chapter 3, statistical significance implies that a f is unlikely to have arisen by chance. The less probable it is that the diffe due to chance fluctuations, the more confident one can be that th difference between the groups. A 'p' value of .05 or less ('p<.05' the likelihood of a result arising by chance is approximately 5 other words, it is 95 per cent likely that the difference reflec probability of .01 suggests that the likelihood of the differ by chance is 1 per cent, and it is 99 per cent likely that scores. A probability of greater than .05 is usually implies that chance could have played a role in t'

3. This statistical test (analysis of variance) is r one group is different from the mean leve' extent than expected by chance. In eff groups are compared, because the sp there is between the groups. If there standard deviations) the means will ha different from each other.

6 Use of Sanctions

The preliminary discussion in Chapter 5 has shown (Table 5.1) that two-thirds of the offences alleged against the sample of reoffenders in 1992 resulted in a conviction and sentence at court, while 11 per cent resulted in a caution. In the remaining cases, the charge was dropped or withdrawn or still pending, or no police action was taken, or the young person was found not guilty. This chapter considers in more detail the pattern of sanctions, including both cautions and sentences, with respect to these offences.

Figure 6.1 sets out the range of options that were open to the courts in dealing with these reoffenders.

The use of cautioning
Given that this sample represented the 'higher end' of juvenile offending, the majority of the offenders in this study will have already been arrested and charged by the police for other offences before the start of 1992. From their own accounts, half had been arrested by the age of 12, although these probably count as 'arrest' some incidences that were not treated as such by the police. After the first arrest, the cautioning rate for subsequent offences is not very high. Fifteen per cent of known offences committed by these reoffenders in 1992 resulted in a caution.

In relation to this sample, cautions were used most frequently for four in offences; 37.2 per cent of these 423 cautions were for various types heft (excluding theft of or from cars), 7.3 per cent were for road traffic ces, 9.2 per cent were for criminal damage and 8.7 per cent were for bodily harm. Much concern has been voiced about the possible e of 'multiple cautioning'. It is not possible to present a full picture of cautioning in relation to these reoffenders, as data was collected ne year. However, only 17 per cent of reoffenders received more ution in 1992 (see Table 6.1).

Figure 6.1   Main orders and sentences of the Youth Court

Supervision orders These orders may be made on offenders aged 10-17. There are several different types of supervision order, of which the following are the most common:

– a supervision order with a residential requirement;

– a supervision order with a requirement to undertake specified activities – 'intermediate treatment';

– a supervision order with requirements to undertake or to refrain from certain activities;

– a supervision order with educational requirements.

Attendance centre orders Such orders may also be made on 10-17 year-olds where attendance centres are available. Orders require attendance at a centre for two hours of activities up to a maximum of 24 hours for 10-15 year-olds and 36 hours for 16-17 year olds.

Community service order A CSO may be made on 16-17 year-olds up to a maximum of 240 hours. Like an ACO the court must be satisfied that provision is available.

Probation order The Youth Court may now sentence 16 and 17 year-olds to probation if it is considered more suitable than a supervison order. The same group are also eligible for the combination order (community service and probation) and the curfew order.

Conditional discharge The condition of the discharge is a specified period of time to a maximum of three years. During this time, if the offender appears in court for a subsequent offence they may be charged with the original offence as well.

Fines Limited to £1,000 for anyone under the age of 18.

Custody There is now a single sentence of detention in a young offender institution which may only be used for those aged 15 and above. In doing so the court must be satisfied that:

– the offence, or the combination of the offence and one other associated with it, was so serious that only such a sentence can be justified for the offence; or

– where the offence is a violent or sexual offence, that only such a sentence would be adequate to protect the public from serious harm.

These criteria may be waived if the offender refuses to consent to a community sentence. In addition, custody is available (in the Crown Court) for any offender aged 10-17 who commits a grave crime such as murder or manslaughter.

Table 6.1   Number of cautions per offender

Number of cautions	Number of offenders	(Per cent)
0	326	(61)
1	115	(22)
2	62	(12)
3	24	(5)
4	3	(1)
5	1	(-)

Pattern of disposals
Table 6.2 lists the range of disposals used by the courts in dealing with the offences committed by these reoffenders in 1992.

Non-custodial sentences (excluding cautions)
As Table 6.2 shows, the non-custodial sentences given by these courts formed the majority of disposals. A total of 2,557 out of 2,885 offences (90 per cent) resulted in a non-custodial sentence ranging from a fine to a conditional discharge of over a year. In addition, reflecting the fact that a small number of offenders turned 17 years old during the year and thus became eligible for probation, probation orders were given for a small group of offences (n39). The most frequent non-custodial sentence was a supervision order, with or without extra specified activities. Supervision orders were given for 636 of the offences, a total of 22 per cent of the full range of offences. In a few cases, offenders were simply bound over to keep the peace without any separate penalty, and in one case the usual court disposal was that the offender should be 'detained within the premises of the court for one day'.

Custodial sentencing
A total of 289 disposals involved a custodial sentence, which represented over 10 per cent of the total known offences. The majority of these sentences were for a period of three months or less. On only eight occasions were sentences of longer than six months in a young offenders institution (YOI) given by the court. Custody was most frequently given by the courts for car theft and road traffic offences; together these accounted for 45 per cent of the custodial sentences. Twenty-two per cent of these custodial sentences were given for burglary. Altogether 56 reoffenders (approximately 10 per cent) had received custodial sentences in a YOI during 1992.

Table 6.2   Disposals of offences in 1992

Disposal	Number of offences receiving disposal	(Per cent)
Cautions		
Caution	423	(14.7)
Non-custodial		
Fine	83	(2.9)
Compensation	49	(1.7)
Community service order	57	(2.0)
Attendance centre order (<=12 hours)	146	(5.1)
Attendance centre order (12+ hours)	300	(10.4)
Supervision order (<=1 year)	279	(9.7)
Supervision order plus* (<=1 year)	140	(4.9)
Supervision order (>1 year)	116	(4.0)
Supervision order plus* (>1 year)	101	(3.5)
Conditional discharge (<=1 year)	387	(13.4)
Conditional discharge (>1 year)	73	(2.5)
Probation order	39	(1.4)
Detained for one day	1	(0.0)
Bound over to keep the peace	3	(0.1)
Custodial		
Young offenders institution (<1month)	76	(2.6)
Young offenders institution (1-3 mth)	140	(4.9)
Young offenders institution (4-6 mth)	65	(2.3)
Young offenders institution (>6 mth)	8	(0.3)
Other		
No separate penalty	341	(11.8)
Not known	58	(2.0)
Total	2,885	(100.2)

* Supervision order with specified activities

Note
The use of the code of 'no separate penalty' tends to vary between courts and districts; in some cases, the criminal record printout will list disposals separately for all offences, even if they are all to run concurrently with each other, whereas in other places the printout will simply indicate 'NSP'. These 'NSP' disposals are likely to be fairly evenly distributed across the range of disposals and the absence of these offences from the subsequent categories should not substantially bias the results. Only one disposal was counted for each offence. Where there were several, the heaviest was counted. This means that the table slightly understates fines, which tended to go with other, heavier, sanctions.

Table 6.3 **Number of different types of disposal tried with each reoffender in 1992**

Number of different types of disposal tried with each offender in 1992	Number of offenders	(Per cent)
One type	26	(5.4)
Two types	235	(49.0)
Three types	169	(35.2)
Four types	2	(0.4)
Total unknown	48	(10.0)
Total	480	(100.0)

Types:

1 Caution

2 Community (including community service order, attendance centre order, supervision order, probation order)

3 Fine (sole sanction, including compensation)

4 Custody (in a young offenders institution)

5 Other (bound over, detained for one day, etc)

6 Conditional discharge

Range of disposals given to defendants
Table 6.3 shows that even within one calendar year, when it was unlikely that many young reoffenders would have been sentenced more than twice, the police and courts tried several different disposals with them, ranging from cautions, through community-based options, to custody.

Progress through the criminal justice system
The recording of dates of offences, dates of arrest and dates of court appearances made it possible to calculate the number of days that it took for each different offence to be processed through the youth justice system.

Time between offence, arrest and court
Table 6.4 shows the average time that it took after the offence was committed, before the offender was arrested. In the majority of cases, arrest was immediate, but in a minority of cases, it took a relatively long time before the police were able to arrest their suspect.

Table 6.4   **Time (days) between offence, arrest and court according to police files and court records***

	Mean days	(SD)	n**
Days from offence to arrest	6.6	(20.8)	2421
Days from offence to court	97.8	(68.3)	2557
Days from arrest to court	86.0	(67.7)	2407

*   excluding cautions, pending, cases dropped or dismissed
**   numbers vary slightly because some offences are missing one of the three dates

Table 6.4 also shows that on average the final court trial was heard approximately three months after arrest.

Offenders' perceptions of the time from offence to sentencing
Criminologists, police, legislators and others are frequently concerned about the knowledge and understanding of the criminal justice system demonstrated by young offenders. An assessment of their knowledge was made by asking reoffenders how long it would take for a hypothetical offence to get to the point of sentencing. These estimates ranged from 'immediate sentencing' to 10 months, while the mean was 2½ months. Since the mean length of time that it took for their offences to reach court in 1992 was three months, their beliefs appeared to be that the system was working slightly faster than it was.

Summary
The majority of the reoffenders in this sample had already been charged with an offence before the start of 1992, although hard information on these earlier charges is not available. The relatively low rate of cautioning in this sample reflects the fact that these were not, for the most part, first offences. There was little evidence of multiple cautioning within the year. The majority of offences were tried at court and resulted in a community-based sentence, usually a supervision order. Approximately 10 per cent of these offences resulted in custodial sentences, and only 8 offences out of a total of 2,885 known offences resulted in custodial sentences of longer than six months. It took an average of over three months for offences to be sentenced, but offenders themselves estimated that offences would be tried in less than three months.

7 Other Aspects of the Reoffenders' Lives

A considerable amount of existing work on offending by young people has focused on the individual characteristics and family backgrounds of young offenders, in the hope that this will help identify the causes and correlates of such behaviour (Wadsworth, 1979; West, 1982). Because self-report studies showed that most children were engaged in offending at some stage in their lives, some argued that research on the individual and family characteristics of offenders was relatively fruitless. The issue of reoffending refocuses attention on such work, however, for although *most* young people may engage in criminal acts at one time or another, persistent offenders by any definition are a small minority.

Although the response rate among the more frequent offenders was low, and the sample interviewed was very small (74), the survey still provides a unique source of illustrative information about a group that is very hard to interview. This chapter considers the results for the 74 interviewed. The penultimate chapter describes the case histories of 7 individuals in greater detail. In addition to the interview data, the present chapter relies on the data collected from social services records of 230 young people in the full sample who had such a record.

Relationship with family and care histories
A number of previous studies have looked at the family backgrounds and family size of young offenders and, in particular, at the experience of family disruption (Wadsworth, 1979; Farrington, 1983). The children interviewed as part of this study were asked a number of questions about their current living arrangements and relationships with family members and friends. At the time of the interview, 22 reoffenders were living with both parents (parent indicating biological, step or parent's partner or, in one case, grandparents), 32 were living with their mothers only, 5 were living with their fathers only, and 15 were living with neither parent.

When asked whether there was a mother or father (or mother/father figures) with whom they had some contact, the interviewees reflected a lot of contact with their mothers in particular, even if they were not living with her. Only 4 young reoffenders were without any parental figures in their lives.

It was very rare for these children to report that they did not get on with their mothers. Nine out of 10 interviewees said that they either got on very well or fairly well with their mothers; the remaining 10 per cent reported that they either got on badly with her, or they did not have enough contact to measure the quality of the relationship. However, despite this, they did report quite a lot of relationship change over recent months. Half of the sample said that their relationship with their mother had changed since the previous year, most of these reporting that they had grown closer (33 per cent of interviewees). Given the usual pattern of adolescent relationships with parents, and considering the fact that this sample were frequently in (serious) trouble, these findings seem a little surprising. The interviewers reported that of all the sections of the interview, this was the one where they felt that they were not getting a full picture. They attributed this to the likelihood that the children felt a strong maternal loyalty, and seemed reluctant to 'tell tales' about her to a complete stranger asking personal questions. One interviewer wrote, 'The saddest moments were asking him about his relationship with his parents, he became withdrawn and I thought he might cry, although he maintained that everything was OK'. This section came quite early in the interview, and was not so obviously related to the original stated aim of inquiring about juvenile offending and youth justice. It is also possible that, despite extensive reassurance, they had not quite convinced themselves by this point that the interviewers were nothing to do with social services. Many had experience of care, and were possibly suspicious of social workers.

However, despite their reservations about the truthfulness of respondents' answers about their relationships with their mothers, in several cases the interviewers reported strong evidence for very close relationships. The following comment from one interviewer was not untypical of what they included in their written reports: 'He's obviously close to his Mum, and his Mum obviously cares a great deal about him'. In another case, it was commented that, 'Craig seems very pleasant, and showed a lot of respect for his mother'. The mothers themselves contributed to the discussion occasionally. One mother took particular exception to what she viewed as the generally negative slant of the questioning in the interview schedule, and wanted to know why everything was so 'anti': 'Why don't you ask how many times a month he buys me flowers?' she asked, 'or how often he smiles?'.

They were only slightly less loyal to their fathers. Fewer interviewees had a father figure, 1 in 4 stating that there was no such person in their lives.

Of the 55 interviewees' 'fathers', 84 per cent were reported to be biological fathers, and 16 per cent were grandfathers, brothers, or step-fathers. In 8 out of 10 cases where there was a father figure, it was suggested by the interviewees that they got on very or fairly well with these men. Again, they reported a lot of relationship change, with half of the interviewees saying that they were getting on better or worse in 1993 than they had in 1992. However, in contrast to their reports of their relationships with their mothers where they had said they were growing closer, they said that they were growing apart from their fathers. In one case we have assessments of their relationship from both the son and the father. The son was interviewed in a young offenders institution, and reported that he was 'fairly close' to his father. Keen to give us his side of the story, his father wrote to us saying, 'In truth, I've secretly been a nervous wreck for years... why [does] he persistently choose to shame his father, whilst also making [me] more ill in the process?'.

There were other suggestions, in answer to later questions, that things were not as rosy as the interviewees were suggesting. Half reported that they had run away from home at some point, for at least a night, and often for much longer. In several cases, children had run away for months; in one of the case studies presented in Chapter 8, a 12 year-old boy had slept 'on the streets' for over three months. This matched the information gathered on children who could not be interviewed; it was not unusual for parents or social workers to comment that these children had run away or had not been seen for several weeks.

Questions about relationships with parents recurred at different parts of the interview, and later questions also hinted that the initial positive reports were not strictly accurate, or at least did not apply to the whole sample. At separate points in the interview, interviewees were asked whether their parents disapproved of their friends in any way, and also whether their drinking and drug habits had caused difficulty for them with their parents. In many cases the responses tended to suggest that there were several things about the way that they were leading their lives that their parents openly expressed disapproval about. In 70 per cent of cases, their parents had disapproved of either all or some of their friends ('Why did I put so much effort in,' wrote the father cited above, 'only to have him finally desert me in favour of his so called friends?'). Of those interviewees reporting that they drank alcohol, one quarter also reported that this caused family problems, and a similar proportion reported that they had had trouble with their families over their drug-taking habits.

In addition to the answers to the interview questions from the 74 interviewees, the social services information on all those who had had some contact provides a different perspective on the family backgrounds of these young reoffenders. It was ascertained that of those 230 reoffenders 'known' to the social services departments, 6 per cent were *currently* on the Child Protection Register. Although this represents only 2.5 per cent of the sample of reoffenders as a whole, it underestimates the proportion of children who have been on the Child Protection Register at *any* stage in their lives.

A separate way of approaching the question of familial disruption was to look – for all 230 children with social services contact – at the number of different episodes of social services care that they had experienced during the course of their lives. In fact, this is accurately recorded for only the Midlands children (n196), where counts of different periods in different types of accommodation give some flavour of the amount of disruption and discontinuity they had experienced. Previous research referred to above (Farrington, 1983; Thorpe et al, 1980) has indicated that a disrupted family background significantly increases the chances of young people becoming offenders, and these data give some indication of the amount of movement and change experienced by some of the children. Of the 196 known to social services in the Midlands, 28 per cent had experienced 10 or more different places of accommodation during their lives, and over 10 per cent had 20 or more episodes recorded by social services (the highest number recorded was 64). Some of these placements or episodes will have involved being placed back with families they had lived with before, or will be extensions to periods in children's homes where they were already living, but even with this proviso, these numbers suggest a great deal of disruption in care during the childhoods of many of these young people. Indeed, 21 children had more than five separate placements in 1992 alone.

The question inevitably arises as to whether the disruption is the consequence of offending behaviour, or whether the disruption comes from general familial difficulties. Of course, the two are intertwined, but it was possible to collect basic information from the Midlands social services concerning the reasons that all interviewed or not interviewed children first came into contact with the local authority in the Midlands county. Once again without going through all the individual files, which would have taken months of work, it is not possible to very specific. Table 7.1 shows the 'reasons' for first coming into contact and distinguishes between supervision orders, care orders, being accommodated compulsorily[1] and being accommodated and maintained under voluntary arrangements[2].

It is possible to make a rough and ready distinction between routes into care that more commonly result from offending or other disruptive behaviour, and routes that are more commonly associated with welfare

Table 7.1   Reasons for first contact with social services: Midlands reoffenders only

Type of first contact	Number of reoffenders	(Per cent)
Supervision order	18	(9.1)
Accommodated compulsorily	18	(9.1)
Care order	28	(14.3)
Accommodated and maintained	127	(64.8)
Other	5	(2.6)
Total having contact with social services	196*	(99.9)

*   189 Midland's reoffenders had had no contact with social services

problems. Children accommodated as a result of a supervision order and some of those accommodated compulsorily will have been referred because of disruptive behaviour, whereas those accommodated as a result of care orders and those 'accommodated and maintained' will more often have been referred because of social welfare problems. Table 7.1 shows that the first involvement of only 9 per cent of those known to social services was as a result of a supervision order, with a similar proportion being accommodated compulsorily. Thus, at a rough estimate, 18 per cent of those known to social services first entered the system because of their offending behaviour. The great majority probably came to the attention of social services because of social welfare problems. Some examples are given in the case studies in the next chapter. There are some difficulties in presenting these figures arising from the fact that the Children Act of 1989 was implemented in October 1991, implying some changes in terminology and the recoding of information already on official files. Due to the implementation of the Act, the care order in criminal proceedings was abolished, but some of these in the sample with care orders recorded against them from prior to 1991 may have entered care by the offending route. The 18 per cent is possibly an underestimate.

This passage below provides an example of a social services' account of the lives of one of the reoffenders (not interviewed):

> B. comes from a distressing and chaotic family background. His mother is a registered drug addict and heavy drinker. She lives with her cohabitee who is also renowned for his abuse of alcohol and drugs. B's father left the family when B was 5 and is now uncontactable somewhere abroad.

From all reports B's first 5 years were reasonably stable and happy. However, the lifestyle of his mother and her partner was entirely unsuitable for B. They are completely undisciplined. They often had no food in the house, had no daily routine and were renowned for domestic disputes and violent behaviour. B and his sister were primarily responsible for their own welfare both at home and at school. B's own unpredictable behaviour and negative traits in the face of unstructured situations is clearly a direct consequence of his experiences at home. In 198x, the decision was taken to remove B and his sister from their home on the grounds of their development being avoidably impaired. B has never accepted his enforced separation from his mother and refuses to understand that she is incapable of caring for him.

Friendship groups

On the whole, the interviewees seemed to be a sociable group. Unless they were spending time with their own partners, the majority of them spent much time with their peers. Only 5 per cent claimed to see their friends less than once a week, and most saw them much more frequently, 72 per cent claiming to see them more than six days a week. The nature of these friendship groups varied, sometimes involving groups of four or more (36 reoffenders), sometimes involving two or three people (30 reoffenders), sometimes just one other person (8 reoffenders). Perhaps surprisingly, approximately half of these reoffenders were part of friendship groups consisting of both boys and girls. They tended to socialise with people of their own age or older, only 6 per cent having friends who were younger than them.

As would have been expected, it was usual for these offenders to get into trouble with the police in the company of friends. Over 80 per cent of reoffenders reported that this had happened at some point. These figures indicate a higher level of co-offending than those extracted from the police data, probably because the police data pick up only offenders who were actually arrested. Frequently, the police witness accounts will report that others were present but escaped. As already established from the police data, most of the offending within these groups involved car theft, non-residential burglary and road traffic offences. However, interviewees were also asked whether they got into fights with their friends, such as fights in the street, in pubs or at football matches. Over half said that they did get into fights, but only 1 in 10 did so in the company of their regular friends.

This suggests that, for some offences, the offenders were acting on their own, or with others perhaps not considered to be friends, or going 'out on a limb' in some way. In order to find out whether these offenders were sometimes acting outside the general rules of behaviour of the group, they were asked if their friends ever disapproved of things that they did.

Surprisingly, a large proportion – a third – reported that their friends did not always agree with what they were doing.

School experiences

Two out of three reoffenders had opted out of school by the time they were interviewed, in many cases before the official leaving date. In several cases, the interviewers relayed the general message that they had managed to leave school at a very early stage, and that the schools had done nothing to pull them back. There were several accounts within the group of mothers battling with the local authorities in order to get the child taken back into another school. Frequently the reoffenders reported that once they had been excluded or suspended from school (one in three temporarily excluded, over half permanently excluded), nothing subsequently happened. One reported that no one from the school had come round to the house for four years after he had left. Of course, our own interviewers' experience was that it was extremely difficult to 'call at the houses' of these families, and often messages that someone had called were not passed on. However, whatever the circumstances, it was not unusual to be told that in some way the educational system had failed these young people.

Whether they were still attending or not, all interviewees were asked about their school experiences, and these were, not surprisingly, fairly negative. Forty per cent reported that they disliked school, and a further 20 per cent were neutral. Two out of three had been involved in fighting at school, the same number were frequently in trouble with the teachers.

One fifth felt that their school work was below average, and the same proportion claimed some problems specifically with reading. Although perceptions of performance and actual performance can be at variance, an overlap between juvenile offending and reading problems is frequently reported in the research literature (eg. Ouston, 1984, who found that 'non-delinquents' scored higher than 'delinquents' on a variety of reading tests). Fourteen of the 74 reoffenders said that they had had remedial help for reading difficulties. And yet, despite the fighting, the suspensions, the exclusions, and their reading problems, they still felt that qualifications had a role in their future lives. When asked about how far they would like to take their education, over half hoped to have exams from school, or go on to college after school. And yet two-thirds already claim to have left school.

Their aspirations were also at odds with their truancy rates; truanting, and offending whilst truanting, were both common. Sixty-six out of 74 had had truanted, and in 1992, over half of the group had missed one month or more of their schooling. Half of these had missed a term or more. Two out of three of those who truanted admitted to having offended whilst truanting.

This divergence between the reoffenders' current educational situation and their aspirations may have two possible explanations. It is possible, on the one hand, that even though their alienation from the formal educational system is fairly complete and, despite their criminal activity, they retain conventional views of the avenues through which they can improve their lives[3]. On the other hand, it is also possible that the children were just repeating formulaic answers to a question that was of little relevance to them – there is some evidence, for example, that thinking about the future is an activity young offenders engage in sparingly (see, for example, Willis, 1977).

Whatever the reality, and it is difficult to do more than speculate, it remains the case that for a large proportion of these children the formal educational system was part of the their past rather than their present and, consequently, it is difficult to see how it was going to become part of their future without enormous input. The government proposal that persistent young offenders should receive an educational input as part of a secure training order would appear to be essential, and to have any chance of having an impact this will need to be extremely intensive. The following report from an educational support services head describes the exceptional efforts needed to engage children of the kind included in this study in the educational process.

> At the risk of seeming arrogant if it wasn't for the total input I give T it would be impossible to retain him (at the school). I base this opinion on eight years of experience in dealing with children in difficulties. By total input I mean the extra time I devote to ensuring that he doesn't become frustrated or over-excited and precipitate problems with his peers and other teachers. This necessitates me arriving in school by 7.15 am every morning and planning the activities for the day. I spend every break and lunchtime in the Support centre with T and his group and I have opened the room to other pupils at this time. In this way the pupils in my care retain social contact with their peers in a controlled situation. At the end of each day T and I discuss how things have gone and then I phone his key-worker. Due to the open and honest nature of my dealings with him, he hears what I am saying to (the key-worker) and I'm sure he knows how much we both want him to be successful and to stay out of trouble. On the occasions when he is going straight home, I write a note, usually one of encouragement to his parents. He has proved that he can be trusted to deliver these and so help his parents and I to maintain contact. Therefore, he is under my constant supervision at all times he is on the school site. I believe this to be the foundation of his success. He enjoys coming to school as he feels he is achieving positive results. Also, he now has an excellent record of attendance. A restricted programme offers the safety, security and support he needs.

Current financial support

As reported in Chapter 3, a substantial proportion of the reoffenders were not doing anything at the time of the interview. Several interviewees discussed the problems of finance and independent living. They often cited poverty as a reason for offending. One of the girls in the sample had been frequently arrested for shoplifting from Mothercare. Despite an increasing aim by government departments that parents should extend financial responsibility until children are aged 18 or even 21, some of their parents were of the opinion that having turned 16, these young people should be supporting themselves. However, very few were in employment, and if they were not working and were living at home, they were ineligible for any sort of state financial support. Their employment and financial futures did not look positive. The Cambridge Study of Delinquency suggested that by the age of 18 frequent offenders were more likely to have erratic work histories including periods of unemployment, and were more likely to be living away from home (thus needing money to support themselves).

Alcohol and drug use

Several recent general surveys of schoolchildren have suggested that use of alcohol and drugs is widespread and rising. Discussing results from Gallup/Wrangler (1992) and from the Schools Health Education Unit at Manchester University (Baldwin, 1991), Mike Ashton of the Institute for the Study of Drug Dependence recently wrote:

> Although the rise of LSD and ecstasy may be the highlight, there appears to have been a trend towards greater variety in youth drug use, with the emphasis on stimulants and hallucinogens but with cannabis also being used in a wider variety of situations' (Ashton, 1993).

Preliminary results from research underway at Manchester University (Measham, Newcombe and Parker, 1993) reported that over a third of a cohort of 776 14 and 15 year-olds had tried drugs with high rates of hallucinogen (LSD) and stimulant use, as well as cannabis. Fifty-nine per cent of the cohort had been offered drugs. However, only 1 per cent of the cohort had tried cocaine, tranquillisers and heroin.

Alcohol and drug use were widespread amongst the 74 young reoffenders interviewed. Only 4 had never tried alcohol, a rate of 5 per cent compared to 14 per cent of schoolchildren who had not tried alcohol in Manchester University survey. The numbers of reoffenders having tried alcohol was thus not very different from what is reported in broader surveys of schoolchildren, but it would appear that their use was heavier than the norm for this age group. Three-quarters of the reoffenders drank alcohol regularly (compared to 30 per cent weekly drinkers in the Manchester study), and the same proportion (though not necessarily the same people) also claimed to have been 'really drunk' at some point. These results also confirm the conclusion of the Cambridge Study of Delinquency that offenders drank more beer and got drunk more often than non-offenders (Farrington and West, 1990). Seven of the sample reported that they were getting drunk more than once a week, and five said that they were drinking every day. In several cases, offenders claimed to have drunk alcohol heavily, for a short period of time. For example, one 13 year-old boy said that he had given up drinking, having drunk heavily for a period in the previous year.

Reflecting the impression from surveys that drug use is becoming more varied amongst young people, the reoffenders who were interviewed admitted to a high level of familiarity with a wide range of drugs. Again, however, their use was heavier than that reported for representative schoolchildren. Three out of four had tried cannabis at some point, compared to one in three of the schoolchildren in the Manchester study. Forty-one per cent had also tried something else. Table 7.2 summarises the proportions of people who had tried a range of different drugs, and also shows the frequency of use in the last month. If other drugs had been tried, the most popular choice was hallucinogens, which over a third had taken. A third had also taken amphetamines (33 per cent). These two groups of drugs were also the second and third most frequently reported by the Manchester schoolchildren, offering validity to these findings. Hallucinogens and amphetamines were followed in frequency by sniffing glue or other substances (23 per cent), ecstasy (16 per cent) and cocaine (11 per cent). Several interviewees claimed to have taken drugs or used substances that were not on the self-report list; these included amyl nitrate, butane gas, and petrol. They also included a clinical anaesthetic (Ketamin) that had been recently highlighted in the press as a new appearance on the teenage drug scene. A non-existent drug ('Semeron') was included in the list to check for any tendencies to simply report they had tried everything, but again validity was confirmed by the fact that only one child claimed to have tried it.

Drugs were used at home as well as out with friends. Interviewers reported evidence of drug use whilst visiting these homes. In one case, the interview was interrupted when the mother of the 15 year-old boy came in to collect some cannabis that he had bought for her. One interviewee claimed to be using LSD every other day (see Case Study 6 in the next chapter). Another interviewee, seen in custody, reported smoking a lot of cannabis after 'lights out', in order 'to keep sane'.

Table 7.2   Interviewees' self-reported drug use

Drug type	Ever tried		If ever tried, frequency of use in last month	
	n*	(Per cent)	Mean	(SD)
Cannabis	55	(74)	14.9	(12.8)
Tranquillisers	5	(7)	0.7	(1.0)
Barbiturates	8	(11)	1.4	(2.7)
Amphetamines**	24	(32)	2.9	(3.8)
Hallucinogens (LSD)	29	(39)	2.8	(3.8)
Ecstasy	12	(16)	1.7	(2.4)
Sniffing (anything)**	17	(23)	0.4	(1.1)
Cocaine	8	(11)	0.9	(2.3)
Crack	4	(7)	0.2	(0.4)
Semeron***	1	(1)	0.0	(0.0)
Heroin	4	(5)	0.7	(1.2)
Something else	12	(16)	0.9	(1.5)

*   Two people missing all responses, total n = 72
**   Three people missing this particular response
*** Non-existent drug included as a lie-detector

Some reoffenders reported difficulties not only with their families over drug use, but also with their friends. Eleven per cent had experienced some problems with friends over some aspect of their use.

Psychological health and use of services
Distress, sadness, general stress and lack of social support were common amongst the interviewed group. Half of these reoffenders reported that they had been referred for some sort of counselling or psychological help. The reasons for referral were varied, and the contacts were with various kinds of services. In some cases they were with educational psychologists, in others with psychologists who were part of the prison service or the local authority. Help was sought for drugs problems, for fighting, for 'anger', for depression, for offending behaviour, and for school exclusions. In 19 cases, young people reported experience both of psychologists and also of other forms of counselling. One girl had been told by her boyfriend that it was 'either the drugs or him' and had sought help from her general practitioner. On another occasion, she had also been referred by the doctor

for anorexia, and on a third occasion she had seen a counsellor whilst she was resident in a children's home. She thought that the last had been organised by a social worker and the police. Apart from cases like hers, referrals for some form of counselling were often the result of action on their mothers' part. The educational system also played a role, and in one case an offender reported that the counselling had been arranged by his solicitor.

Reactions to counselling amongst the interviewees were mixed. Some reported that it had been helpful, others that it had not 'worked'. Others had difficulty with the commitment, and said that they had only gone once and then never tried it again – fairly common reactions to initial experiences of counselling.

Offenders' views on their own offending

It was not difficult to get these reoffenders talking about their theories about why people got into trouble, and what might help. Even with the most withdrawn and inarticulate respondent, these questions struck a chord. The four main open-ended questions about offending were, 'Why do some kids your age get involved in crime?', 'And is that the reason you got involved?', 'What stops people from doing it?', and, finally, 'Is there anything or anyone that you think might help you keep out of trouble?'.

There was a high level of agreement in their responses, with few surprises. The first and second questions, concerning reasons for people getting into crime, provoked several general responses. The first was the boredom theme, hence 'Because there's just not enough entertainment around anywhere these days. Some just do it for the fun of it.' In some cases, specific instances where privileges had been withdrawn had led to boredom which had led to offending; one child, for example, had been banned from the recreation centre. The financial gain was a significant response. Many of these respondents said that they did it because they had no money. They needed this money for a variety of reasons, including to support themselves and others ('just hungry'), to go out, and to buy drugs. As one respondent replied, 'The draw, the drugs, you start to love it and then you go onto speed and then you want more and more.' Emphasising the poverty of their backgrounds, one interviewee said, 'It's not often that you can run around a shop and choose what you like'.

Apart from boredom and financial gain, another clear theme was excitement. Certain crimes were associated with 'the buzz' in particular; these were the car thefts, and sometimes the burglaries. Thus, 'I get a buzz out of TWOCing', and 'When I find money in a house, it's a big buzz'.

Another clearly emerging theme was the role of others in pulling them into offending. 'The children's home made it worse', one said, 'I was the youngest, and I learned a lot about TWOC'. 'Mixing with the wrong crowd', said another, and this was frequently repeated. Sometimes it was not just mixing with the wrong people, but wanting to prove themselves to the others. 'I *wanted* to follow the wrong crowd', one reflected, and another commented that 'People who don't get into trouble are cowards'. A third said, 'You like to follow the leader and be as big as your friends'. Looking 'hard' in front of the crowd was important, the consequences were not a consideration.

What stops people? Commonsense, paranoia, experience and growing up. People stop if they are 'people who have sense, and realise things are going wrong and want to do something before it is too late'. 'They learn', another said, 'that crime isn't a good way of living'. Fear of the consequences, not considered at the initial stages, begins to seep in, thus, 'mine is a paranoia, I'm paranoid of going to prison. The policeman told me about [YOI], I don't fancy going there'.

They begin to have more experience of the police and courts, and 'being arrested and slapped in a cell is not very nice. People who keep going aren't bothered about such things'. Sometimes it is just time: 'When you are over 18, that's it, you should stop'.

Others think the answer to the question is nothing. 'I'll never stop, nothing will make me stop taking drugs'.

And was there anything that might help? The response to this was overwhelmingly that certain people might help. Mums, Dads, sisters, girlfriends and boyfriends all featured strongly. 'I've got too much too lose', said one respondent, who had a steady girlfriend. 'My gran encourages me not to do things, and it's always in my mind, but I still do it. I see my gran a lot.' There were some practical responses, some reasonable, some not. One respondent claimed he would stop if someone would give him '£800 for nought' to replace the £800 he was earning through crime. Another suggested that it would help if he could have a motorbike to drive. 'I just want to have something constructive to do', said one incarcerated interviewee, 'I always wanted to be a bricklayer – something to focus the mind'.

General impressions during interview

One of the main impressions gained from the interviews was the absence of any particular 'type' amongst these reoffenders. They came from a range of backgrounds, lived in variety of different types of home, and gave a number of different accounts of their lifestyles. However, there were some themes that emerged from the interviewing and although such information can only be impressionistic, it may illustrate some of issues that emerge from the statistical analysis elsewhere in the report.

The most frequent comment by interviewers about the respondents was that they were pleasant. For example, one interviewer wrote, 'I'd been round a couple of times before, but no-one had told him about the study, and I was actually on the doorstep as he was coming in from work. He took me straight in and made me a coffee, and got straight on with it. He seems to be sorting things out for himself now, and he has got a job.' Many were reportedly 'friendly and cooperative'. Thus, 'He is a nice person and was truly cooperative and obviously doted on his baby brother', or 'Extremely hospitable, mature, cooperative, and remorseful'. On one occasion the interviewer commented 'surprisingly polite and respectful. He asked me if it was OK if he smoked – I was stunned that he had asked'.

As the converse to these positive statements, interviewees could also be passive, and difficult to engage in the task of answering the questions ('untouchable', the interviewers commented). They sometimes gave an impression of a lack of introspection and a reluctance to reflect or think about their lives from a distance. A short attention span proved a challenge in some cases. For example, one interviewee fell asleep several times during the interview, something which he could achieve during anything over a five second break in the conversation.

A sub-group of the interviewees were proud of their offences, and showed a lack of remorse when recounting their actions. Several, it was felt, were living up to their image. In the whole group of reoffenders, three had been approached by television companies making documentaries on juvenile offending and one interview refusal was based on the disruptive effect of an earlier television interview. However, it was equally common for the young people to suggest that they did not find their offending particularly enjoyable, but that they felt they were somehow caught up in it.

The impression of chaotic lives gained from reports of children who were not interviewed was occasionally replicated in the lives of those who were seen. On one occasion, the interviewee was arrested by the police in the middle of the interview, and after a chase up the street, was taken away in a police car, leaving the interviewer in mid-sentence. During an interview in a children's home, the interviewer commented 'as the interview wore on, he became fairly destructive – pulling the putty out of the window frames, tearing all the pictures off the wall, ripping his trainers up – he was still quite friendly to me though. Although he was quite small, he obviously liked to 'play the hard boy', but on the occasions he smiled, he still seemed very young.' During another interview in a children's home, another child in the home threw a tantrum, kicking the windows and screaming. The interviewees main objection was that this other boy was 'a scruff', and had not cleaned his teeth that morning.

The fairly high frequency of dramatic events in these children's lives is reflected in the interviewers' accounts; children often had scars and reported hospital admissions for accidents, crashes and stabbings. In one case trauma counselling had been offered to a boy after a particularly serious stabbing. Several interviewees had had parents who had committed suicide, one at least had had a sibling killed in an accident. One family in the sample (two sons met the reoffending criterion) was being subjected to vigilante behaviour by neighbours, which included, their solicitor claimed, having their garage destroyed and visitors come to the door with weapons.

Corroborating this impression from the interviews of lives containing disproportionate experiences of loss, social services files also contained many such stories. Hence, this report of a family of a reoffender.

> The family was referred in 198x by the educational welfare service. All three children were poor school attenders. K and his brother were also causing concern because of their acting-out behaviour – jumping off roofs, crossing dangerous railway lines, travelling on trains without their parents' knowledge. Though social workers had been involved fairly continually with the family for a couple of years there was intention later in the 1980s to close the case as the boys' offending appeared to be decreasing. However, that year their mother was told she had terminal cancer and she died eighteen months later. The brothers' offending escalated after their mother had first been told that she was dying. The offending escalated again after her death, although it had always been a problem. There was strong likelihood that the boys would be received into care after their mother's death, though this was resisted by their father, though it appeared to social workers that he wasn't coping. Within a year the boys and their father moved in with his new partner and her children. Two years later he was jailed for 14 years for an extremely serious intra-family criminal offence. The boy's offending has continued unabated.

Summary

Our impression of the lives and backgrounds of these young reoffenders is likely to be affected by the fact that it was easier to interview offenders who were at home with their families. Because many of those seen were still at home, their accounts of their relationships with their parents are likely to be better than those who are not at home, for had the relationships totally broken down, the young people would be more likely to have left their parents' house. Nevertheless, within this sample of 74 interviewed reoffenders, not all were seen at home, and a proportion were interviewed in independent living or in custody.

Generally, they reported close relationships with their mothers, although there was other evidence of family discord over drug use and friends. They spent a great deal of time with their friends, and the majority did not have any full-time occupation of any kind, relying instead on families and offending to support them. School, for most, had been a negative experience, and several still had reading problems. However, even in the face of major school difficulties leading to substantial truancy and early departure from the educational system, many retained traditional images of a future with educational qualifications and professions.

Whilst we would be wary of drawing conclusions from such a small group, it should be noted that the evidence of disruption and loss in their lives, together with their lack of education and their experience of psychological or counselling intervention are all far from typical of adolescents as a whole.

Notes

1. 'Accommodated compulsorily' means living in local authority accommodation usually because of a residence requirement of a supervision order, being on remand for trial or sentence (Children and Young Persons Act 1969), or being under an emergency protection order (including s.53 of the CYPA 1933).

2. 'Accommodated and maintained' includes foster placements, children's homes and other community placements including schools.

3. There are several examples of this in the accounts contained in Graef, 1992.

Part III

Persistent Young Offenders?

8 The Issue of Persistence

Introduction

It is now well-established that at any one time there is a small proportion of offenders that are responsible for a disproportionate amount of criminal activity (Wolfgang, et al, 1972; West and Farrington, 1977; Home Office Statistical Department, 1985; Farrington, 1987). Not surprisingly, the existence of such a group has led policy-makers and, occasionally, researchers, to speculate about the possibility of achieving a marked impact on offending by focusing attention on the activities of these high-rate offenders. The most frequently voiced approach is based on the assumption that locking up or taking 'out of circulation' these 'high-rate offenders' will lead to a substantial drop in crime. Such views have been expressed on a regular basis in the popular press. Under the headline *'The Untouchables'*, the *Daily Star* of 30 November 1992 suggested that

> ...hardcore child super-crooks are bringing fear to Britain's streets... they are our number one crime problem, tearaways just out of primary school who have learned their lessons in motor theft and housebreaking so well they account for **90 PER CENT** of offences [emphasis in original].

In a similar story, the *Daily Mirror* on September 9 1993 quoted a Chief Superintendent from the West Midlands Police saying that if he had the powers to lock up the six most persistent young offenders in his area 'it would cut his car crime by up to 40 per cent'.

The bulk of this report so far has focused on a sample of reoffenders all of whom were arrested a minimum of three times during the course of one year. They can for the most part, therefore, justifiably be considered to represent the 'heavy end' of juvenile offending. Indeed, one study (cf. Tarling, 1993: Appendix 2) has suggested that fewer than one in five young offenders are dealt with three times or more by the police before the age of 17. Obviously far fewer will be dealt with three times or more in the course of a year. Throughout the report the individuals within this sample have been referred to as 'young reoffenders'. There are two main reasons for this. First, it is to distinguish them from the bulk of young offenders who neither offend nor are arrested as frequently. Second, it is to distinguish them from what is believed to be a smaller group – generally referred to as 'persistent offenders' – whose offending is believed to be significantly more frequent than the majority of reoffenders. The extent to which it is possible to identify a group of 'persistent' offenders within this sample is the subject of this chapter.

The core issue is how might such a group be defined? Is there some straightforward basis on which these individuals may be identified and are the offending patterns of these individuals recognisably different in some important respects? This chapter explores the implications of using three different definitions of persistence. It highlights a number of difficulties with the proposed policy in relation to persistent young offenders:

◆ no two definitions of persistence will lead to the identification of exactly the same individuals;

◆ the fact that a discrete group of persistent offenders cannot be identified in this manner suggests that any definition of persistence will tend to be arbitrary;

◆ the sentencing of juveniles on the basis of a definition of persistence will therefore involve a degree of inequity;

◆ provision for persistent offenders is therefore likely to be targeted inefficiently.

Defining persistent offending

There are a number of ways in which 'persistent offending' may be defined. Perhaps the most obvious is simply by frequency of offending. Frequency of offending may also be measured in a variety of ways. First, frequency of arrests can be used as an indicator of offending. Second, frequency of known offending (either including or excluding TICs) is perhaps the most logical measure, though frequency of known and alleged offending or, for the purposes of research, frequency of self-reported offending, could also be used.

In this chapter three quite different definitions of persistence are used and the sample of young reoffenders analysed using each in turn. Henceforward they are referred to as *definition one, two* and *three*, and they are set out in Figure 8.1. *Definition one* – in fact a set of three related definitions – involves identifying the most persistent young offenders (10-16 year-olds) in the sample according to frequency of arrest, number of known offences, and number of alleged offences. The frequency of self-reported offending is a separate issue, as it is much higher than official records for the whole sample, and may well be unreliable in a number of

---

Figure 8.1   Definitions of persistence

Definition one
Frequency of offending in one year

All those children aged 10-16 who appear in:

– the top 10% of children arrested most frequently, and

– the top 10% of children with most 'alleged' offences, and

– the top 10% of children with most 'known' offences.

Definition two
Frequency of offending in a three-month period

All those children aged 10-16 who are known or alleged to have committed ten or more offences in a three month period.

Definition three
Possible new secure training order criteria

All children aged 12-14 who commit three or more imprisonable offences, one of which must have been committed whilst subject to a supervision order

- and where -

the offence under consideration must be serious enough to warrant a secure training order.

---

ways. Similarly, given the unreliability of the TIC figures, they are in the main excluded from these analyses, though some observations with TICs included will occasionally be offered.

The two other sets of analysis presented in this chapter are based upon definitions of persistence used by the Home Office. The first of these is the definition utilised in the pilot research undertaken by the Home Office (described in Chapter 1). In this work, 'persistent offenders' were defined as those juveniles (again, 10-16 year-olds) who were known or alleged to have committed 10 or more offences in a specified three-month period. The final definition is that which it appears likely will be used as the criteria for determining eligibility for the secure training order. The definition used here is the commission by someone between 12 and 14 years of age of three or more offences punishable by imprisonment, one of which was committed while the offender was subject to a supervision order. This is slightly narrower than the criteria contained in the Criminal Justice and Public Order

Bill which also includes those children who have committed three imprisonable offences and are found to be in breach of a supervision order.

Using these various definitions, this chapter will examine how many and which young reoffenders from our sample would fall under the rubric of 'persistent young offender'. Having identified the groups – assuming that it will not always be the same children that are being identified – this chapter will examine the experiences and characteristics of the individuals who are so defined, and will compare them to the broader group of children arrested three times or more in 1992. Finally, the implications of this for the current Home Office policy of secure training orders will be examined.

Definition one: persistence defined by frequency of arrests and offending over a year (10-16 year-olds)

Beginning with definitions that arise from frequency of offending, popular commentary frequently focuses on the most active 10 per cent of offenders in terms of numbers of arrests or numbers of offences. Despite the fact that any such definition is essentially artificial, examining the top 10 per cent nevertheless allows popular views of offenders and offending to be examined in some detail and, in so doing, enables some conclusions to be drawn about whether those who are arrested or who offend most frequently (at least according to official records) are different in some significant way from the rest of the sample of young reoffenders.

However, in order to overcome some of the potential shortcomings of taking an arbitrary cut-off point, the analyses below are based on the overlap between three different measures of persistence. Thus, taking the 10 per cent most frequently *arrested* offenders within this sample group of reoffenders who had all been arrested three times, gives a group of 47 reoffenders, the cut-off being more than eight arrests in one year. By contrast, taking the 10 per cent with the greatest number of *offences* attributed to them, gives 51 offenders who have 14 or more known or alleged offences against their name in 1992. Finally, using *known* offences only, the top 10 per cent gives 51 offenders with who have 12 or more known offences to their name.

Because each of these numbers of most persistent offenders represents 10 per cent of the pool of 531, they are very similar; 47, 51, 51, the differences being caused only by the fact that, in some cases, it is not possible to split the pool precisely at the 90:10 location. However, although the numbers are similar, the key question is that of whether or not the same people are being identified using each of the definitions? A count was performed on how many reoffenders met the criteria for frequency only on one, only on two or for all three of these variables. Table 8.1 shows the

Table 8.1 **Numbers of reoffenders meeting persistence criteria for arrests, known and alleged offending**

Number of criteria met by offender	Number of offenders	Per cent of total group of reoffenders*
Meets one criterion	19	4
Meets two criteria	20	4
Meets all three criteria	30	6

* The total is 513; 18 do not have data allowing these calculations

results, and demonstrates that 19 reoffenders were persistent according to only one of the frequency criteria, 20 reoffenders according to two of the frequency criteria, and 30 according to all three. Given that the variables on which they were measured were all related to the same original incidents, the overlap is probably as high as it will be in any sample. Even by these closely related criteria, therefore, different children are defined as persistent depending on which measure is chosen.

The 30 offenders who are persistent by all three criteria represent 5.6 per cent of the original sample. As such, they are the most frequently arrested young offenders in the Midlands county and in these two London boroughs in 1992. There were no other juveniles in the study areas arrested and successfully charged more frequently than these 30. It is probably fair to assume, therefore, that these are the juveniles in whom the police, the courts, the press and the public are particularly interested. What can be learnt about them from the data collected in this study?

Three of them are girls. This ratio of girls to boys in this most persistent group is not particularly different from that found in the overall pool of reoffenders arrested three times or more, where it was approximately 1:7[1]. The difference between the ratio of 1:10 girls in these persistent offenders, and the original ratio in the overall group of reoffenders, is not statistically significant, but the numbers are really too small to draw any firm conclusions. Nevertheless, the findings seem to support our earlier suggestion that if girls cross the threshold and become fairly frequent offenders, they will offend at similar rates to boys. If they were offending less frequently than the boys, overall, then the ratio of girls to boys would have dropped considerably by the time we looked at very persistent offenders. This group were more likely to be known to social services than the full sample. All but one of the 30 were known, two of whom were currently on the child protection register.

Three of these 'persistent' offenders were from the London areas, and 27 from the Midlands area. Approximately a quarter of the original pool came from London, so this suggests that there were slightly fewer persistent reoffenders in the original London group than there were in the Midlands group. However, one of our earliest findings was that the Midlands offenders tended, as a whole, to have more offences attributed to them than the London groups, and it is likely that this will reflect differences in local police and court practice rather than a lessened likelihood of persistence in London. The difficulty with this definition, as with any definition based on officially recorded offending, is that it will not necessarily reflect some 'real' underlying rate of offending, owing to procedural differences in dealing with offending (cf, Blumstein and Cohen, 1979).

These more persistent offenders were fairly evenly spread across the age range, apart from a slightly larger number of 15 year-olds (9) compared to the other year groups. They were as likely to be 12 (5) as they were to be 13 (6), 14 (4) or 16 (5), a somewhat more even distribution than that in the sample as a whole. There was only one 11 year-old in the group of 30, and no 10 year-olds. These 30 offenders were arrested an average of 13 times in the year, and were successfully cautioned for or charged with an average of 22 offences each. In total, this group of persistent offenders (the most persistent 6 per cent) accounted for 760 alleged offences between them in 1992, of which 663 were known. This group of persistent young offenders accounted for approximately a quarter (23 per cent) of all known offences committed by the whole group of 531 offenders.

Were the offences that they were committing any different from those committed by the full sample of young reoffenders? The four most common offences in their total of 663 offences were car theft (20 per cent), road traffic offences (19 per cent), non-residential burglary (11 per cent) and criminal damage (9 per cent). The rarest offences were grievous bodily harm (0.3 per cent), sexual offences (0.3 per cent), drugs offences (0.6 per cent) and possession of weapons (0.3 per cent). Thus, the distribution of offences was much the same on this definition as for the whole group, for whom burglary, road traffic offences and car theft were also amongst the most common offences. It is not the case that these persistent offenders were committing the more violent or serious offences in the pool, whilst the remainder were committing less serious ones. This is not to underplay the seriousness of road traffic offences and car theft, of course, but merely to emphasise that their occurrence was not confined to this subset of offenders.

Although, as we have suggested on a number of occasions, the data collected on TICs need to be treated with extreme caution, in relation to this group they do appear to reinforce the impression that these are the most 'persistent' offenders in the sample. In the sample as a whole, only 31 per cent of offenders had any TICs recorded against them during the year. By contrast, among this subset of 'persistent' offenders, 80 per cent had TICs. There were over 550 TICs attributed to the 'persistent' group as a whole, an average of 19 offences each. Not only were this group more likely to have TICs, they also had a greater number of TICs each.

Definition two: persistence defined by frequency of known and alleged offending over a three-month period in 1992 (10-16 year-olds)

This section, using a different definition from the first, makes comparisons not only between the two groups of persistent offenders – looking at the numbers identified, and frequency and type of offending – but also between the persistent offenders and the main sample. In its own pilot work on the issues, the Home Office defined persistent juvenile offending as all juveniles under 17 who were known or alleged to have committed 10 or more offences in a three month period, namely April to June 1992. This definition includes offences taken into consideration by a court which, as we explained above, we have tended to exclude from our analyses because of the unreliable nature of their recording in the police files. We will continue to exclude them from our analyses in the main part of this discussion here, since where we do have them, they relate only to the Midlands sample and would therefore bias the results towards the Midlands reoffenders. In addition, they were not always given precise dates. The effect of including TICs is briefly considered below. We have also tended to exclude alleged offences from our analyses, but for the purposes of comparison with the Home Office will include them in this section.

Taking the same criteria as the Home Office (apart from exclusion of TICs), and looking at exactly the same time period, we find that eight reoffenders were known or alleged to have committed ten or more offences in those months of 1992, in one Midlands county and two London boroughs. In addition to this our data, however, provide information about the other three quarters of the year, as well as the quarter investigated by the Home Office. Table 8.2 presents the results for all four quarters of the year, indicating which individuals met the criteria in each or every quarter of the year. From this we can see that while eight reoffenders met the criteria in the second quarter, 14 did so in the first quarter, 17 did so in the third quarter and none did so in the last quarter[2]. The table also shows that it was rare for these individuals who met the criteria in each quarter to be the same individuals. Although there were 14 individuals in the first quarter, 8 in the

Table 8.2   Individuals committing 10 or more offences (not including TICs*) within each quarter of 1992

ID	First Quarter	Second Quarter**	Third Quarter	Fourth Quarter	Individual's total no. of appearances
8009			x		1
8023			x		1
8052	x				1
9042	x				1
9059	x				1
9097		x			1
9124			x		1
9135		x			1
9137			x		1
9159			x		1
9172			x		1
9240	x	x	x		3***
9248	x				1
9251	x		x		2
9253		x	x		2
9257			x		1
9259		x			1
9304			x		1
9305	x	x	x		3****
9312	x				1
9318			x		1
9335	x	x			2
9337	x				1
9345	x				1
9357			x		1
9358	x		x		2***
9360	x				1
9379			x		1
9395	x	x			2
9428			x		1
Totals 30	14	8	17	0	

*   TICs were not included because it was not always possible to date them (there were over 1,900 altogether). In addition, because of their skewed distribution, they would introduce a significant bias; if TICs were introduced in court, they tend to be in large numbers, but they are not evenly distributed across the sample. This may be partly to court practices, police recording practices, or other reasons. Excluding them is likely to give a more realistic picture.

**   Period used in Home Office pilot research on persistent juvenile offending.

***   Currently in a young offenders institution.

**** Left a young offenders institution recently.

second and 17 in the third, in only two cases were these the same individuals. In a further five cases, individuals met the criteria in two of the quarters. In fact, over the whole year, 30 individuals are caught offending 10 times or more in these three-month periods.

There is quite an important point to be made here. It tends to confirm the belief that offending, particularly persistent offending by juveniles, is a relatively transitory activity. This has implications for attempting to determine the number of persistent young offenders operating at any particular time. Clearly, the longer the period of time that is used as the basis for investigation, the greater the number of persistent offenders that will be identified. This simple exercise suggests that calculating provision or policy on the basis of one time period runs the risk of underestimating the numbers of people who offend this frequently. It is possible, of course, that within any one quarter, those children who offended frequently will receive a custodial sentence and so will not feature in the calculations for the following quarters. This was the case in relation to six individuals in this sample. Of these six, three reappeared in a subsequent quarter after their period of custody, and the other three were in a YOI in the last quarter of the year. The two individuals who offended 10 times in three of the quarters of the year both had very recent experience of young offenders institutions.

The 'persistent young offenders' according to this definition had a total of 742 known and alleged offences attributed to them in 1992. If the figure is recalculated to exclude alleged offences, the group had 575 known offences attributed to them, this representing a fifth (20 per cent) of all known offences committed by the reoffenders in 1992. Each of these persistent offenders was arrested on average 11 times during the year, and had approximately 24 known and alleged offences (of which 19 were 'known') attributed to them. Almost 70 per cent of the group had recorded TICs against their name during the year. A total of over 600 TICs were attributed to this group, an average of 22 each, figures very similar to those recorded for the first of the groups of persistent offenders.

The offences attributed to them were, once again. not markedly different from those committed by either the full sample or those defined as persistent using the previous definition. The three most common offences in the total of their offences were road traffic offences, car theft, and non-residential burglary. The least common offences were drugs offences, possession of an offensive weapon, GBH, and prostitution. Violent and other very serious offences were rare.

The definition of persistence in this section is based on a shorter time period than the definition used in the previous section. How do the 30 individuals identified as fairly intensive frequent offenders within three months relate to the 30 offenders identified as fairly frequent offenders over the period of the whole year? Fifteen individuals appear on both lists. Once again, different definitions of persistence give quite different results. Thus, for example, of the *most* persistent offenders (that is, the two offenders who appeared in three of the four quarters, see Table 8.2), only one would have been defined as persistent using definition one. Similarly, not all of the five offenders who appeared in two quarters would have been identified as persistent using the first definition.

The above analyses, in order to be directly comparable to the Home Office pilot study, included alleged as well as known offending in the definition of persistence. In all the other definitions being used here, however, alleged offences are excluded as being potentially misleading. What happens, then, if alleged offences are excluded in this case? First, and not surprisingly, fewer offenders meet the criterion of 10 or more offences in one quarter. Using known offences only, seven persistent offenders were recorded in the first quarter, four in the second quarter and 11 in the third quarter. No offenders appeared on all three occasions and only three on two occasions. Finally, one further comparison. In order to attempt a strict comparison with the Home Office pilot survey, the data on offending (including TICs) were re-analysed in order to identify those individual who were known or alleged to have committed 40 or more offences during 1992. It was not possible to divide the year into quarters as the offences that were taken into consideration could not be accurately dated. A total of 23 offenders in the Midlands sample (5 per cent) were identified according to these criteria. On average, these 23 individuals had committed 71 offences each in 1992 of which 48 had been TICd. Interestingly, only 13 of these 23 persistent offenders were also identified as persistent when TICs were not used in the analysis.

Definition three: persistence defined by the proposed criteria for the new secure training orders (12-14 year-olds)
The recent response by the Home Office to the issue of persistent juvenile offending was an announcement to introduce 'secure training units'. These, it is understood, will be accompanied by 'secure training orders' which will have their own threshold criteria by which persistence is to be judged. A key exercise in this research, therefore, was to attempt to apply those criteria to this sample of young reoffenders with a view to calculating how many would be eligible during the course of one year for a secure training order. It also allows, of course, a further comparison to be made between different definitions of persistence. The definition used here is any juvenile aged

between 12-14 who has committed one imprisonable offence whilst subject to a supervision order, and who has committed two other similar offences.

Before beginning to discuss the results of the analysis using this definition, a few caveats must be entered. First, ours is a selected sample of more frequent offenders, not of all offenders. Consequently, it is possible that there may be offenders who are on supervision orders who meet the criteria, but who were not arrested three times in a year. This possibility becomes all the more likely if it is possible for the three imprisonable offences criteria to refer to one incident out of which three or more charges arise, that is, where there has been only one arrest occasion. If the three imprisonable offences have to be committed on separate occasions, this would reduce the chances of there being many offenders who would meet the criteria but who are not included in this sample. One problem with taking offences committed on one occasion is that this does not necessarily imply that the offender offends persistently. This is offset somewhat by the fact that if they are subject to a supervision order, this should imply – assuming they will be likely to have at least been cautioned for earlier offences – that they have been arrested on several different occasions for different offences. However, the data collected in this study suggest that the offences that lead to the supervision order may occur up to a year prior to sentencing, again challenging the idea of 'frequent' serious offending.

The second caveat is that this study can provide information only on offending over one year. That is, there may well be some offenders who have committed three imprisonable offences whilst on a supervision order imposed sometime during the previous year, but that one or more of these was committed prior to the period being studied here. In this way we may once again underestimate the number of persistent young offenders according to this definition.

Finally, as we understand it, sentencers, when considering the new disposal, will be asked to ensure that the offence under consideration is *serious enough* to warrant a secure training order. It is difficult for us to make any judgement about how this might be applied, but it is important to note here that it is likely that only a proportion of those identified as potentially eligible (having committed three imprisonable offences while subject to a supervision order) will be eligible in practice for a secure training order.

Approximately 1 in 20 of the sample of young reoffenders[3] would, on the basis of what happened to them in 1992, appear to have been eligible for a secure training order had the sentence existed. A total of 25 offenders aged 12-14 committed one imprisonable offence while subject to a supervision order, already having committed two other offences previously.

These 25 offenders represent 5 per cent of the overall sample, compared with the sub-samples of 6 per cent constructed using the other definitions.

Excluding TICs, these 25 offenders between them had a total of 423 alleged offences attributed to them in 1992, of which 316 were known. These 316 offences represent less than a tenth (8 per cent) of all the known offences committed by the reoffenders in 1992. On average, children identified as persistent by this last definition had 16 known and alleged offences attributed to them, of which 11½ were known. In addition, they were arrested, on average, 7½ times in the course of the year. Finally, we have evidence of a total of approximately 440 TICs being attributed to these offenders during 1992. By contrast with each of the groups discussed above, only 64 per cent of this group had recorded TICs, an average of 16 each. By each of these measures they appear to be less 'troublesome' than those identified by other means[4]. Thus, they committed many fewer known offences on average, and were arrested on fewer occasions and had marginally fewer TICs attributed to them. Once again, however, the offences committed by this group were similar in many respects to those noted in relation to the previous sub-samples. Road traffic offences remain the most frequent (18 per cent), followed by non-residential burglary and car theft (16 and 14 per cent respectively). ABH and other types of assault accounted for 3 per cent of cases, and there were no successful prosecutions for GBH among this group.

There is one final, but extremely important point to be made in relation to this final group of persistent offenders. It is that there appears to be relatively little overlap between this group and the other two groups – considerably less overlap than there is, for example, between the first two groups where half of the offenders were persistent according to both definitions. In order to compare the definitions, it was necessary to restrict the age range for each to 12-14 year-olds only, so that the first two definitions are tested on the same pool of children as the third. In addition, because the third definition could only be applied to children in the Midlands sample (where we had full information on supervision orders) it was also necessary to restrict these calculations to Midlands children only. The whole sample of reoffenders contained 193 children aged 12-14 in the Midlands county. Of the 25 eligible for a secure training order, only 4 were defined as persistent according to definition one, and 7 according to definition two. Because of overlap between these cases, in total only 8 of the 25 offenders identified by definition three were defined as persistent according to either of the other definitions. Finally, only three offenders out of the total sample of 193 Midlands 12-14 year-olds were identified as persistent according to all three definitions.

The final section in this chapter consists of seven case studies, each of which gives some flavour of the types of offenders that have been described above as persistent according to one or more of the definitions used.

Case studies of interviewed persistent young offenders

A total of seven reoffenders who met at least one of the criteria for persistence described above were interviewed. In one case, the child met all three criteria, and was one of only three children in the whole group to do so. One of the children was in a young offenders institution, one in a local authority secure unit, and five at a family home of some description at the time they were interviewed.

Case one
(Persistent according to *definition one* and *definition two,* interviewed at home)
At the time of interview, John was a 14 year-old boy. He had been 12 at the beginning of 1992, and was thus one of the youngest frequent offenders. He had 15 known offences on his record for 1992, including theft from shops, ABH, and criminal damage. He also had one case of arson, and three burglaries (unclassified), several pending cases and at least five offences that had been taken into consideration by a court. Of the two cases of criminal damage on his record for 1992, one had been for damage at a children's home, and one for damage to a police transit van. He sometimes offended with his brother, or with others in our sample of frequent offenders, who were older than him. The police tended to bail him for offences, but on several occasions in the year they had kept him overnight in the police station. He was under a supervision order for the second half of the year and had already committed a burglary and a theft by the end of the year, so he was also approaching the criteria needed to meet our third definition.

He was still attending school at the time of the interview, and living with his father and his brother. He had been there for a year and a half. Although John didn't live with his mother, he had some contact with her and knew that she was unemployed. His father was also unemployed. He reported that he got on 'fairly well' with his mother, and 'very well' with his father. He had never run away from home. He had spent time in a children's home, where he reported that he got on 'OK, I did make friends'. John was under a supervision order, and reported that his social worker 'has been very helpful with everything'. However, he said that care 'was horrible because there's no-one you can talk to or anything'. He did not like being physically restrained, and felt that the staff were too old. From the children's home, he 'went on the streets' for 3½ months, joined by his younger brother for three weeks. He slept in an attic at a 'rave' for one night, otherwise he slept 'on the streets, in the market, anywhere'. In the end the police picked him up, and he was taken to a police station and looked after by a member of staff. Being on the streets 'was still better than being in the children's home, I don't know what it was there, I just didn't like them'.

John likes school, and hopes to go to college to be a car mechanic. He truants regularly, and has done throughout secondary school. During 1992, he estimated that he missed more than a full term of school. He has been excluded from school for fighting, and was then sent to a special school or unit where he is now.

His peers have been a problem. He met his friends in care, and they were older than him. He sees them more than six times a week, and when he was in care he used to get into trouble with the police with them. He reported that he was first arrested when he was 9, for putting a Tesco's trolley through a shop window. When asked for the causes of his offending, he said 'Because I was in care, and I knew that I wouldn't get into trouble. I used to enjoy robbing and TWOCing but I don't anymore'. Why do people stop? 'Because they get bored of it, or they go home'.

His recent health has not been good; he has had bronchitis. His mother sought psychological help for him, through concern for his fighting. This was several years previous to the interview, and he still sees the counsellor every few months, but does not feel that it has done any good. When asked how satisfied he was with his life, he replied 'Better than before'.

The (male) interviewer, wrote that,

> Of all the people that I have met, this one makes me the saddest. His stories about being on the street nearly made me cry. I know you can't really tell by such things, but he looked to have the world's sadness in his eyes. His father's house is actually really well sorted out, I've been there a couple of times, and it is scrupulously clean and there are always piles of freshly ironed clothes and he is always cooking – I wish I knew what had happened to cause such pain.

John's social services care history hints at a lot of disruption over the past couple of years, corroborating John's accounts of times spent in children's homes. He was first taken into care a couple of months after his twelfth birthday, when he was placed in a fairly large children's home, in another town from that where his parents lived. Within two months he was moved on to another children's home, then back to his father in the middle of 1992 for five months. Subsequently he was moved to a third children's home for one week, and on to a fourth home for another three weeks, then to his mother. He cannot have stayed here long, since we saw him back with his father. In addition, he was on the child protection register.

Case two
(Persistent according to *all three definitions,* interviewed at home)
The second child we interviewed who met the frequency persistence criteria was a 16 year-old boy, Phil. He had been 14 at the start of 1992. He had 17 known offences on his record for 1992, including robbery, several burglaries, handling stolen goods, and driving offences. He also had alcohol and drug offences; he received an attendance centre order for possession of cannabis. He had one case of aggravated TWOC, committed with others well known to us. He had been convicted of stealing an electric drill from British Telecom, cash and cigarettes from a students union, of handling stolen suitcases, a camera, and a Barclaycard. His range of offending was obviously broad.

At the time of the interview he had left school for the summer, and was working full-time, although he intended to return to college in the autumn. He was living with his mother, his father having died 10 years previously. They had been in their current home for five years. His mother was not working. His relationship with her was good, and he reported that they had grown closer over the last year. Phil said that he had run away from home when he was 13 for five or six days, and had also spent time in a children's home, during the summer of 1992. He was only there for one week, and felt that he had got on well. He had also said that he had been on remand in a young offenders institute for two weeks, and hated that.

Phil had started playing truant from school when he was 11. He had left his first school before they expelled him, and was subsequently expelled from the second. These exclusions had been for fighting and bullying, and he was referred to a special school or unit, and as well as a school based psychological service. He still fights with people at school, and gets into frequent trouble with the teachers.

Currently his main social contact is his girlfriend, whom he sees everyday. His other friends are older than him, and he sees them in a group, all male. His mother disapproves of his friends, and up until seven or eight months ago he got into trouble with the police through his friends. Relationships with the police are not good, unsurprisingly. He claimed that a policeman had dislocated his shoulder several months previous to the interview when he had been charged with drunk driving.

When asked about his first arrest, Phil said that he was nine years old, and 'led astray', shoplifting. He claimed that he offended for money. He reported that he had not committed any offences for eight months, although he had been 'an expert burglar', earning £500 a week. The interviewer reported that his mother attributed his offending to the death of his father when Phil was seven, but Phil did not agree. Whether or not people stop offending was due, in his eyes, to 'how much help they get, through Mum, social workers, probation'. He feels that they all helped him. Apart from this, when asked what would keep him out of trouble, he replied 'myself'. The courts, he felt, were very good to him. 'They kept on letting me off saying, sorry Phil, this is your last chance, and then still not putting me away'. In addition, he said that he was 'in love'. His view of the future involved settling down with and marrying his girlfriend.

He drinks five pints every night, is very drunk more than once a week, and has had definite problems with his family and his friends over drinking. He claimed to have used a variety of drugs including marijuana, amphetamines, hallucinogens, ecstasy, and cocaine. He had also had serious family and friend problems over this. He too had been referred to a psychologist, through the efforts of his mother, after her GP had suggested it.

Phil was known to social services, although his care history only showed one contact, in the middle of 1992, when he was recorded as being 'in care' but placed with his mother.

Case three
(Persistent according to *definition two*, interviewed at home)
The third very persistent offender was 15 at the time of the interview, and so had been 14 throughout 1992. He had 12 known offences on his record, and a further two that had been dismissed at court. He too had a broad range of offending, beginning the year with residential burglary and ending with TWOC. His offences included several 'going equipped to steal', when he was equipped with metal piping, screwdrivers, and bolt croppers. He had committed burglary on a school, and had several vehicle related thefts, including theft of an excise licence. He had one case of aggravated TWOC, which had involved him hitting an oncoming police transit van, whilst driving a stolen vehicle. Like the others, he offended with others already in the sample.

He was still attending school and living with his mother, father, brothers and sisters. Both parents were unemployed. He got on fairly well with both of them. He had run away from home four times in the previous year, and had spent time in a children's home, commenting 'I thought it was all right, safe, I made friends there and still see them'. Social services, however, did not provide a care history, indicating that he was not known to them.

His schoolwork is below average, although he had not had any extra help that he remembered. He began truanting when he was 14, and had been permanently excluded for doing so, and also for fighting. He went on to another secondary school. In 1992, he said that he missed more than one full term in total. He frequently fights at school, and frequently gets into trouble with teachers.

He sees most of his friends (who come from around his neighbourhood) more than six times a week, and they consist of a fairly large group of other boys. His parents disapprove of some of them, and he has got into trouble with the police with them. He also gets into fights with strangers, sometimes with his friends. He was first arrested at the age of 11 for using a knife on another boy.

He had little idea why he had started offending, apart from the fact that 'some have brains and know how to do it and others don't'. Prison was a deterrent, and the only thing he could think of that would help was car rallying. He feels that the police hate him, and claimed to have been set up several times, and beaten up on occasion. He said that he was taking a police officer to court for assault in his own house. The courts, on the other hand, were usually 'all right', and tried hard to take the time to make sure he understood.

He drank 8-10 pints a week, usually on one occasion, but this did not cause any difficulty for him. As was very common, he smoked marijuana (every day in the last month), but didn't use other drugs. He had had some counselling about his crime, from social workers and probation officers. Peter was not satisfied with the way things were at the moment. His future in a year's time? 'Bird'. And in five years? 'Settled down, have a kid'.

The interviewer reported that Peter was pleasant and cooperative, but bored and in need of 'kicks'. He was at his most coherent and articulate when describing the lack of things to do, which he saw as a major source of difficulty for him. He has been banned from the community centre, and the youth club has been closed and changed into an arts centre. One youth worker had managed to engage Peter, but, Peter claimed, he had been disciplined for taking too many people in a van, and had given up after that. The interview finished with a general discussion, where Peter reported feeling excited about going to a YOI (he is awaiting trial for four TWOCs and two burglaries), 'it's better than being out here'.

Case four

(Persistent according to *definition one* and *two*, interviewed in a local authority secure unit)

This fourth case, Nick, had just turned 13 at the time of interview, and was seen in a children's home. He had been 11 for the first six months of 1992, making him one of the youngest children classified as persistent by any definition. He had been in the unit for two months, and before this he had been at a different children's home for three months. His 1992 record included several counts of criminal damage, theft from a shop, actual bodily harm and grevious bodily harm, taking and driving away, robbery (of shoes), and setting of a fire alarm at an old people's home. Altogether he had 20 offences for which he had been successfully prosecuted in 1992, and a further five that had not been proceeded with. His record contained no information on TICs.

Initially, Nick was passive in the interview session, but as the time wore on he became fairly destructive, pulling the putty out of the window frames, tearing the pictures off the walls, ripping up his trainers, all the time maintaining a friendly interaction with the interviewer. He was physically small and looked young, but seem to like to emphasise his 'hardness'. The surroundings were not very peaceful either; during the interview another child in the unit was throwing a tantrum, kicking windows and screaming. He said that his relationship with people working in the homes in which he had stayed were sometimes problematic; he had struck a member of staff with a stick on one placement. However, he had made a wide range of friends from his homes.

Before his placements with social services, Nick had lived at home with his family. His mother was unemployed, and his father worked in a factory. He reported good relationships with both his parents, and said that he had never run away from home. He had quite enjoyed school, although he said that he was not attending any more. He was not concerned about the standard of his schoolwork, and was not interested in education in any way. He had truanted from the age of 12, and during the previous year had missed between a month and a term in total. He reported that he offended while truanting, got into fights at school, and had been both suspended and excluded.

His friends were mainly from other children's homes, but he sees little of them in the secure unit. His parents disapprove of them because he is always getting arrested with them. Before custody, he was spending up to £200 a week, but now gets an allowance of about £2. His first experience of the criminal justice system was when he was arrested at 11 for punching a child whose mother called the police. When asked about the seriousness of different offences, he said that although he appreciated that people could be killed by others driving stolen cars, he was himself a very good driver and so there was less danger. He believed that peer pressure was a strong influence on offending, and that mixing with the wrong crowd was what caused people to get into trouble. In addition, a desire to drive before being legally eligible led some to it. Some people might stop offending because they are scared of going to a YOI, but he did not think that anything or anyone would prevent him. Except, perhaps, being given a motorbike, although all his previous ones had broken down. There were only two items on the self-report list that he claimed he had never done – getting into an 18 certificate film and stealing a cheque book or credit card.

Nick drank approximately a dozen bottles of cider in an average week, but rarely got drunk and had not had any problems with others concerning his drinking. In the unit, he does not drink at all. He has used a range of drugs in the past, including amphetamines, hallucinogens, ecstasy and crack. His mother had consulted a psychologist over Nick's behaviour, 'because I'm always hyperactive', Nick said. In addition, a court order had been made requiring him to see a psychiatrist, 'but no one came to see me'.

Nick had only been known to social services for a relatively short time, approximately 18 months, and had had four placements by them with foster families and in children's homes. He was on the child protection register.

Case five
(Persistent according to *definition three*, seen in a YOI)
This fifth case, Carl, had been 14 throughout 1992, and was 15 when seen in a young offenders institution. He had received this sentence subsequent to our trawl through his record; in 1992 his only court disposal (relating to 1992 crimes) had been a supervision order given at the end of the year. Within 1992, he had been convicted of 10 offences, almost all of which were burglaries. They included burglary of cash and jewellery from a house, two other dwelling burglaries, burglary from a squash club, burglary with intent that had resulted in over £1,000 worth of damage. He had been prosecuted for nine 'breaches' of orders of one sort or another including bail. Again, as always, he offended with other high-level offenders known to us. The police bailed him after only one of these arrests; in other cases he was always kept overnight in the police station.

Carl had been in the YOI for nine months previous to the interview, and stated that he had been at home with his family for six years previously. Both his parents were unemployed, and he got on very well with his mother. He hardly sees anything of his father. He said that he had never run away from home, but did admit to having spent time in a children's home. Once, when he was younger, he said, he had been put in a children's home so that his mother could go to hospital, and he was upset because they had tried to stop him from going home to her.

School, as usual, was not good. He openly disliked it, and fought with others in the classes as well as the teachers. He was excluded for fighting with a workman from the council on school premises, and subsequently didn't go back to any school. This happened, he said, when he was 12 years old. However, despite the exclusion, as we found in the sample as a whole, he expressed an interest in some further education, saying 'I would like more education, but I don't know what – I can't learn too much'.

As all these children do, he offends with his friends, and sees them a lot. They are generally older than him, and include girls as well as boys. His parents are not unduly worried about the company he keeps. He and his friends tend to have about the same amounts of money as each other – he estimated his weekly spending at £300. Offending was started 'for money mainly, and for fun', although the amount of fun depended on the offence 'criminal damage, for example, is just mucking about because you've got nothing else to do'. He stressed the financial gain several times, and says that the only reason he would stop would be if his mother 'was getting stress about it'. Custody 'won't do *anything* to stop me'. In the last month, despite being in a YOI, he claimed to have committed a number of offences, including buying drugs every day. He has used, on occasion, marijuana, tranquillisers, amphetamines, hallucinogens, ecstasy, and heroin. Virtually the only drug that he claimed that he had not tried was the non-existent drug included on the list as a lie-detector. Social workers had arranged counselling for him, in order to tackle his offending.

His vision of where he would be next year? 'In a secure unit'. In five years time? 'Settling down with a missus'.

Carl had a long and complicated care history with social services. He had first been fostered when he was six months old, where he had only stayed for two months. A couple of years later, he was fostered again, at the age of two, for a very short placement of a couple of weeks. Four months later he was with a third foster family, where he stayed for a month until just after his third birthday. For two years, he was not in the care of social services, but was taken in again for a period of two weeks covering his fifth birthday and involving three separate families, only one of which he'd been placed with before. Again, a short break ended with him being back with the last family for another couple of weeks, then back to another of the earlier families for nearly a month.

By the time he was 10, he had spent time with nine different foster families on a number of different occasions, as well as spending periods out of care, presumably with his own family. Just before his tenth birthday, he was placed in a children's home where he stayed for over a year, and he was then returned to his mother.

Contrary to his claim to have been with his family for six years prior to his current incarceration, his care history says that in the middle of 1992, he was back in a children's home, and then off to live with his sister for three months. From here he went into a young offenders institution, for two months at the end of 1992. In 1993 he was in another children's home, and, as we have seen, was back in a YOI by the time we interviewed him in the middle of 1993.

Case six
(Persistent according to *definition three*, interviewed at home)
Brian had just turned 16 at the time of the interview, and had been 14 for the first half of 1992. His brother was in the sample as well (a different family to that mentioned above in case four). He had also co-offended with his father; in one case of burglary listed on his 1992 record, four members of the family had been charged. Brian's 1992 offences were serious, but not as frequent as some other offenders; he had been convicted of nine offences, with 10 TICs. Three offences had been withdrawn, including one charge of kicking a dog to death during a burglary. He specialised largely in residential burglary, with one TWOC, and one attempted theft from a vehicle.

At the beginning of the year he had been sentenced to three months in a young offenders institution, and was offending again eight weeks later, immediately on release.

At the interview, Brian said that he had left school and was waiting for college to start. He was living with his mother and his own partner, in the family home, where he claimed to have been all of his life, although in a subsequent interview section he said that he had spent time in a children's home, where he argued with everyone and fought a lot. His mother was unemployed. He got on with her very well, he said.

Unusually, Brian liked school and felt that his work was about average. However, he did not harbour the usual hopes for further qualifications, and was not interested in taking it any further – although at an earlier stage he had said that he was waiting for college to begin. It transpired later in the interview that he had taken LSD recently, and said that he was 'tripping' during the interview. This may account for some inconsistencies in the story. He had played truant from school since the age of 12, and had been temporarily suspended at one point for fighting. He fought frequently, with everyone.

His friends were friends from school, and he saw them more than six times a week. He said, unusually, that he did not get into trouble with his friends and went on to say that while he spent £400 a week, his friends generally had less money than him. Why did people get into trouble? 'Everybody gets into trouble around here', he said, 'there's no particular type... I was bored and I wanted to do it so I did'. Another reason for getting involved was 'so I could get money for myself'. When asked why people might stop, he said, 'because of the hassle of the police and going to court. But YOI only makes you worse'. Personally, he believed that what would help him keep out of trouble were his mother and his girlfriend.

He drinks every day, and gets very drunk more than once a week. This doesn't cause any problems with his mother, but does with some of his friends. He smokes marijuana every day, and takes LSD approximately every other day, and has also tried amphetamines and ecstasy, both of which he had taken in the last month.

Brian was another child with a long and chequered history with social services. His first experience was of a supervision order when he had just turned 14, while he resided at his parents. A few months later he spent a few days in a children's home, and then returned to his parents. He absconded from his parents for approximately three weeks at the end of 1991, when no-one knew where he was. As mentioned above, early in 1992, he spent two months in a YOI, and returned to his mother for a month. Foster care followed this, for a week, then it was back to the family. At the end of the year he spent a week back at the children's home where he had been when he was 14. After another few months with his mother, he was back in a different YOI at the end of the year. Following the YOI, he went back to the children's home, and the last entry on his care history, (which we received in mid 1992) was 'absconder'.

Case seven
(Persistent according to *definition three*, interviewed at home)
This final case, William, was 16 when interviewed. He had five offences on his 1992 record, plus two convictions for breach of a conditional discharge. Two of these were unsuccessful burglaries, in the first case he smashed 16 windows of a school and was caught in the act, and on the second occasion he was caught trying to unplug the video in a house. He also had attempted, unsuccessfully, to obtain cash by deception. On another occasion he had stolen an income support book, and he also had one conviction for criminal damage. Again, he offended with others in the sample, including one who met all three criteria for persistence but who we did not interview. The courts had already delivered a range of disposals;

for these offences he had received a supervision order of 12 months, another of 9 months, a conditional discharge of 12 months and an attendance centre order for 24 hours. He had seven TICs on his 1992 record, three of which were for TWOC.

The interviewer was struck by William's courtesy at the time of the interview, when he was just returning from work. The general impression from the interview was that he was sorting things out for himself now that he had got himself a job. He was working as a car valet, reflecting his general interest in cars. He lived with his mother, brother, sister, and sister's children, at home, where he had been for four years. His mother was working as a cleaner and he had no contact with his father.

School was, reportedly, a neutral experience, he did not report reading problems, but was not interested in taking his education any further either. He had been truanting since he was 12, which had led to the school taking his parents to court, but, unusually, he did not get into trouble with the teachers. In 1992 he had missed up to a third of the school year. He was excluded, for fighting, and was charged with ABH after the incident.

His friends are from the area, and he sees them very frequently, but they did not approve of him stealing cars (they are also fairly new friends, they had changed since the previous year). He does not offend with them, except when he gets into fights, when his friends are always present. Offending is started, he believed, 'because you're not so well off, and have friends who do it, and you lead them on for fun'. He did not actually enjoy stealing cars, but he did enjoy being in them and driving them. What stopped people? 'Growing up, really, and people who don't stop haven't grown up'. He started to stop, 'mainly because of what I was doing to my mum'. Although he claimed to have most of the offences on the self-report list, only two had been committed in the last month. These were buying drugs, and buying something that he knew was stolen. Both of these had been done 30 times.

William only had one entry on his social services care history, which was for the supervision order which he subsequently breached.

Conclusion and summary

It should be clear from the discussion in the main part of this chapter that the most 'persistent' offenders in our sample – whichever of the three definitions was used – did not seem to be strikingly different from the full sample, with the tautologous exception of the frequency of their offending.[5] Thus, they were no more likely to be male, or older, than the full group of children arrested three times or more. Significantly, the types of offence that the persistent offenders committed were similar to those committed by the whole group, including the less persistent. This meant that, on the whole, the types of offence most commonly committed by the persistent offenders in the sample were road traffic offences, car theft and non-residential burglary – very much in line with what was found in the Home Office's pilot research. What it is also important to note is that very serious offences – grievous bodily harm, aggravated burglary, rape and sexual offences – did not represent in total as much as one per cent of all offences attributed to persistent young offenders – a pattern that is typical of juvenile offending generally.

The most serious offences that were committed by any of the persistent offenders on a regular basis, were residential burglary and aggravated TWOC. Residential burglary, for example, represented 3 per cent (17 cases)[6] of all known offences attributed to the 30 persistent young offenders identified using definition two. It is important therefore not to confuse persistence with seriousness. The fact that the vast majority of these persistent offenders commit the same types of offence as the bulk of young offenders, and that they are generally distinguishable only by the fact that they commit them more often, is something that is often lost sight of when discussing possible sentencing practice in relation to this group.

Although the persistent offenders were not distinguishable from the rest of the main sample in terms of their age, gender, or type of offending, it remains possible that there may be other elements of their backgrounds which are different. Descriptive data on their family histories and their drug and alcohol use, were considered in previous chapters, and it is possible that the extremely persistent offenders lead somewhat more chaotic lives than the others in the sample. This was underscored by the difficulty experienced in attempting to interview them. These observations about their lives are reinforced by the data on their contacts with social services. The groups of children identified by each of the three definitions all had higher rates of contact with social services than the full sample of reoffenders, and were more likely to have come to the attention of social services via a supervision order or to have been accommodated compulsorily (see Table 8.3, Appendix 5).

The core purpose of this chapter, however, was to look in rather more detail at the sample of young reoffenders as a whole, and to consider, using a variety of cut-off points, whether there could be said to be a small group of children whose offending patterns appeared to involve much more frequent offending than those in the rest of the sample. Three different cut-off points were used and, consequently, three groups of persistent offender identified. Once identified, the offending rates and patterns of these groups were studied, and compared with those of the larger sample of reoffenders. A number of key findings emerged.

Most importantly, it appears that *no two definitions of persistence will lead to the identification of the same individuals.* The different definitions used in this chapter identified three largely different sets of individuals. Thirty offenders were identified as a result of the application of definition one, and the same *number* as a result of definition two. These first two definitions, although different in some important respects, both attempted to identify the 10-16 year-olds who offended most frequently during a specified period. The first group were identified by listing the top 10 per cent of offenders in the sample, judged in three different ways: number of arrests, number of known offences, and number of alleged offences throughout the year; and then selecting all those who appeared on all three lists. The second definition involved a shorter time-period – three months – and specified 10 known or alleged offences as the major criterion. However, although both methods resulted in the identification of the same number of offenders, only 15 offenders appeared in both groups, while 15 appeared in the definition one but not in the definition two group, and a further 15 appeared in the definition two but not in the definition one group.

The third definition – those juveniles aged 12-14 who had committed three imprisonable offences whilst serving a supervision order – led to the identification of a slightly smaller number of offenders – 25 in all. Even restricting the comparisons to within the age range set by this third definition, and to within the Midlands children only, it was apparent that a largely different group of offenders was identified, there being relatively little overlap with the other two groups. When the age range and area were restricted in this way, the number of reoffenders identified by the first definition dropped from 30 to 13 reoffenders, and that identified by definition two dropped from 30 to 10. Figure 8.2 summarises the number of Midlands reoffenders aged between 12 and 14 (out of 193) coming within each definition, and the number of reoffenders defined as persistent by two or three of the definitions. The figure suggests little overlap between the first and third definitions, although most of the ten children in the second definition do fall into either the first group or third group as well. There was an overlap between which offenders from the first and second groups also appeared in the third group, with the result that only three offenders out of a total sample of 193[7] were identified as persistent according to all three definitions, whereas 36 were persistent according to one definition or another[8].

What is to be made of this? If one of the aims of the exercise is to attempt to isolate that group of juveniles whose offending is appreciably more

**Figure 8.2   Overlap between definitions of persistence
Midlands offenders aged 12-14**

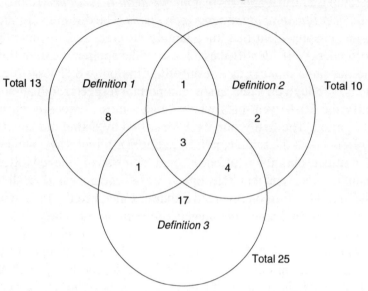

persistent than the majority, the process will have to resolve a number of problems. Each method identifies very different groups. This might be expected if the cut-offs being used were radically different and, whilst the 'secure training order' definition does seem to be dissimilar to the others, the first two definitions (when applied to 10-16 year-olds) might be expected to result in the identification of largely similar groups. The reason that they do not, it appears, lies mainly in the fact that different time periods were used. *The fact that a discrete group of persistent offenders cannot be identified in this manner suggests that any definition of persistence will inevitably be arbitrary.* In using the powers, therefore, sentencers will have to be particularly careful to avoid arbitrary sentencing. If sentencers make secure training orders simply because juveniles meet the legislative definition of persistence, a significant degree of inequity could arise.

The analysis described above in relation to definition two in which shorter time periods of three months were used, also leads to another important point. It is that when calculating the number of offenders in any population that might be defined as persistent, it is important to distinguish between offences and offending, or crime and individuals. Thus, in theory, at any one point, a certain proportion of people will be responsible for, say, 50 per cent of crime. Moreover, it is quite possible that these figures will remain relatively constant. Thus, in January for example, 10 per cent of offenders may account for 50 per cent of offences, and similarly in September, the same may hold true. However, it is highly likely that January's 10 per cent will not be the same people as September's 10 per cent. This point was graphically illustrated in the analysis of offending in three-month periods using definition two. Using this definition of persistence not only was a different number of offenders identified in three separate quarters, but in the main, these were also different offenders. It is crucial, therefore, when discussing the issue of persistence not to lose sight of the fact that it is generally the case that young offenders are at their most active (when they might be defined as persistent according to one definition or other) for fairly short periods of time. Thus between January and September one might witness quite a large turnover of people within, say, the top 10 per cent offenders judged by their frequency of offending. Finally on this point, it is important to bear in mind that given the length of time that frequently passes between arrest and sentence, it is likely that some of the offenders may have ceased being persistent by the time they reach court.

Given what has been said above, and what has been established in other research, it was not surprising to find that a small group of offenders in this sample did account for a disproportionate amount of offending. However, within the sample of young reoffenders the group of most frequently offending reoffenders did not account for an extraordinarily large proportion of offences. Thus, the 30 most persistent offenders according to definition one, who represented the most persistent 6 per cent of offenders, accounted for approximately a quarter of all the offences of the group. A quarter of of these offences is not an insubstantial amount, but it is still much lower than popular estimates of how much recorded crime this small, most persistent group, commit. Furthermore given that this study was restricted to frequent offenders in the first place, this 6 per cent of offenders will account for much less than a quarter of *all* juvenile offending in the two areas in 1992. Thus, for example, the reoffenders in the Midlands sample accounted for less than half (48 per cent) of recorded juvenile crime in the county in 1992. The most persistent group, therefore, accounted for less than 15 per cent of recorded juvenile crime in the County in 1992. The policy implication is, of course, fairly clear. Incarcerating this small group of children for a long period of time would not have nearly such a huge impact on offending as is often claimed would be the case.

In summary, then, not only is the process of attempting to define persistence deeply problematic, but because there is a degree of arbitrariness in the way some offenders rather than others become defined as persistent, creating a custodial sentence for that group raises issues both about equity and about efficient resource use. The issues of equity are mainly to do with the possibility that sentencers might let the inevitable arbitrariness of the legislative definition of persistence follow through into their sentencing decisions. Issues of efficient resource use will arise if sentencing decisions in aggregate result in a poorly and inconsistenly defined group receiving secure training orders. Whilst the research results presented here once again confirm the existence of a fairly small group of juveniles who are responsible for a disproportionate amount of recorded crime, they underline the difficulties which will neeed to be overcome in introducing any measures which impose definitions of persistence in the belief that this will identify a coherent group of individuals that stand in need of special treatment.

Notes

1. Although it should be remember that it varied considerably between the areas.

2. The total number of offences drops quite substantially in the last quarter for the whole group, and this is likely to be due to the fact that information for the end of the year on offending and disposals had not reached the central police files on these reoffenders by the time we were looking at the files in April of 1993.

3. This section is based on the Midlands sample only as we were unable to collect full criminal records for the London sample within the time available. Consequently, it is not possible to determine precisely how many of the London sample were subject to a supervision order during the whole of 1992.

4. Strictly speaking we are not comparing discrete groups, as a proportion of juveniles in one group will be found in one or even both of the others.

5. However, we should emphasise the limited range of variables on which the groups were compared. In addition, comparisons were made over only one year of offending, and further research using longer time periods is needed to supplement these findings.

6. This may a slight underestimate due to the inclusion of some 'undefined' burglaries (which may have been residential) in the 'other burglary' category.

7. As explained earlier in the chapter, it was possible to undertake analysis only on the Nottingham data for the third definition, as full information on supervision orders was collected only in that area. Thus only 193 rather than the full total of offenders could have possibly appeared in all three groups.

8. An analysis of the data using the definition equivalent to that used by the Home Office pilot study (in this case 40 or more known or alleged offences in 12 months, *including* TICs), identified 23 persistent young offenders. The overlap between this final, fourth definition and the previous three is not shown on the diagram. However, as was stated above, 13 of these 23 were also identified by definition two, 10 by definition one, and 6 by definition three. Seven of the individuals defined as persistent by this fourth definition were not persistent by *any* other definition, confirming once again that different definitions of persistence identified different people.

Part IV

General Themes and Overall Summary

Part IV

General Themes and
Overall Summary

9 Summary and Conclusions

Research on juvenile offending has tended to approach the issue from two distinct and often unrelated perspectives. The first begins with offences themselves and, usually via analyses of official statistics, produces a picture of the proportion of offences that can be attributed to young offenders, and enables a description to be drawn of the types of crimes, for which juveniles are prosecuted (inter alia, Radzinowicz and King, 1977). The second approach begins with the individual offender, rather than the individual offence, and seeks to understand criminal behaviour and the development of criminal histories or 'careers' (West and Farrington, 1977; Osborn and West, 1979; Riley and Shaw, 1985). There are few studies which consider both the juvenile offending itself and also the individual offenders, and one of the main aims of this study was to provide more information about the relationship between the two, using a number of different sources of data.

Perhaps the first point to note is that concern about persistent young offenders is not new. At several points during the course of this century, committees of inquiry have been formed to consider how best to respond to the perceived existence of a small group of offenders who offend on a far more frequent basis than the vast majority. The solutions proposed have varied but, generally, they have reflected the alternative approaches of punishment and welfare that have characterised much of the recent history of juvenile justice. Indeed, the identification of a small hard core of persistent offenders is often the justification for the existence of such alternative approaches: crudely put, it is argued that the majority of children are best responded to, at least in the first instance, by an approach that emphasises the need to take account of their welfare, whereas the minority of frequent offenders require more punitive treatment.

This study is best considered in two parts. A significant portion of it is devoted to the analysis of the offending patterns, and experience of criminal justice, of a sample of young reoffenders. These children, all of whom were arrested three times or more in the course of a year, represent the top end of juvenile offending. They are, with perhaps a few exceptions, those children who were offending most frequently in the period being studied. They must not be confused, however, with what are considered to be persistent offenders, as a proportion of them will have committed only a small number of offences in the year. The attempt to define and therefore identify this second, smaller group of persistent offenders, forms the second focus of this report. The two elements are best considered separately.

Young reoffenders
Summary of findings

◆ This study of young reoffenders was conducted in two geographical areas. Analysis of local police files produced the names and records of 531 juveniles (10-16 year-olds) who had been arrested a minimum of three times in 1992. Fewer than one quarter of the sample had been arrested more than five times during the year.

◆ Predictably, boys far outnumbered girls, but in the Midlands sample, girls represented 16 per cent of the sample – rather higher than had been expected, and twice as high as in the London sample.

◆ The most common offences were traffic, non-residential burglary, theft from shops and car theft, in that order. Violence, sexual offences and other serious violent crimes were exceedingly rare.

◆ Self-report data from interviews with 74 reoffenders suggested high levels of unrecorded crime, but of the same types as found in the official records. However, self-report data suggested that there was a high level of drug use which was not reflected in the police records. Arrest for possession of drugs was rare.

◆ Many offenders committed their offences with others, often with other frequent offenders in the sample. Interviewees talked about the importance of others in influencing their offending behaviour.

◆ Many offenders were committing offences while on bail for other offences. Given the frequency of their offending, and the fact that it took, on average, three months for any one offence to be tried, this was not surprising. A third of the offenders had never committed offences while on bail.

◆ The majority of the sentences received by these reoffenders during 1992 were non-custodial. Approximately 1 in 10 offences resulted in custody. Approximately 1 in 6 offences ended with a caution, though no evidence was found of widespread use of multiple cautioning. The full range of disposals were used with this group: supervision orders, attendance centre orders, community service orders and probation orders. Indeed, in many cases the offenders tended to have experience of several different disposals during the course of the year.

♦ Interviews with 74 of these reoffenders suggested that the majority had left school, and many had nothing to do with their time, not being employed or in training or studying. A high proportion of the girls were pregnant or had a child. School had been a negative experience, and many had been excluded from schools, only to leave the educational system permanently.

♦ Interview and social services data both confirmed a picture of severe familial disruption. Half of the sample were known to social services, and the original contact was more likely to be for welfare rather than criminal issues.

♦ Alcohol and drug use were high, and half of the 74 interviewed reoffenders had had some sort of counselling or psychological intervention.

Interviews with persistent offenders

A number of particular difficulties were experienced in attempting to interview the more persistent offenders, and those that we did see provided much illustrative information on a range of issues thrown up by the earlier analyses. Although, when we were able to make contact with them, very few refused to be interviewed, the reoffenders in general and the 'persistent' offenders in particular, were very difficult to track down. The story told by Case one in the penultimate chapter is probably not unusual: at 13 years old, this child had spent over three months on the streets. Tracing such people is almost impossible, and in a few fortunate cases we were able to contact them at home during rare respites from other types of care or absconding.

The seven persistent offenders described in the case studies share many characteristics, although they were also dissimilar in many respects. Their family backgrounds were overwhelmingly chaotic, they had all (except one) spent some time in children's homes, their schooling was usually characterised initially by truancy and ending in permanent exclusion. They all reported high levels of offending, corroborating and extending the police information, and they all reported drug use. There was not a single child in this group who was not using marijuana regularly, and they had all used other drugs as well. However, drug use had only resulted in prosecution in one case in 1992, and prosecution for offences related to alcohol was also rare, although alcohol consumption was high. None of these offenders offended entirely on their own, and most of them were associating with other 'persistent' offenders in the sample, whom they had either met in children's homes, in custody or elsewhere in their local area.

The boys often emphasised the importance of others in their families in keeping them out of trouble or helping them to realise that their offending would have to slow down. Mothers and girlfriends were usually the key factors, and they were not oblivious to the stress that their behaviour caused others. Neither were they, or others, oblivious to their own stress; the majority had had some form of psychological intervention or counselling at some stage. Interviews with these persistent offenders gave the impression of a mixture of chaos, sadness and boredom. What they hoped for in the future was to settle down, have families, and find work. What they saw in the future was usually less rosy.

Persistent young offenders
Summary of findings

◆ The distribution of offences across the reoffenders did not suggest a distinct group of very frequent offenders. Very few frequent reoffenders were identified, and fewer still whose frequent offending continued over an extended period of time. Few juveniles appeared to offend very frequently for more than short periods.

◆ One of the major issues was how persistence might be defined. Three definitions of persistence were used to examine the assumption that there was a small group of persistent offenders accounting for a disproportionate amount of the offences. The first definition was our own, the second taken from previous work by the Home Office, and the last was the proposed criteria for secure training orders. These definitions were then applied to the full sample with a view to comparing the numbers of offenders identified by each.

◆ When applied to the age range 10-16, the first two definitions led to the identification of 30 'persistent young offenders', though these were not the same 30 offenders on each occasion. Fifteen of those identified by the first definition were not in the group identified using the second definition, and a further 15 identified using the second definition did not appear in the first group.

◆ Twenty-five offenders met the secure training order criteria (the third definition). Again, there was little overlap with the other definitions. Only eight of those identified by the third definition, were also defined as persistent according to either of the other definitions.

♦ Only three children out of the full sample of 193 Midlands reoffenders aged 12-14 were defined as 'persistent' by all three sets of criteria, whereas a total of 36 were persistent according to one definition or another.

♦ A comparison between all those meeting any definition of persistence, and the sample as a whole did not reveal any striking differences between the two, with the exception of the frequency of offending. The persistent offenders were not disproportionately engaged in serious offending.

References

Allen, R. (1991) Out of jail: The reduction in the use of penal custody for male juveniles 1981-88. *Howard Journal* 30(1)

Aries, P. (1962) *Centuries of Childhood* Jonathan Cape

Ashton, M. (1993) From cradle to rave – the rise of youth drug use. *Druglink*, May/June 1993, p12

Bailey, V. (1987) *Delinquency and Citizenship: Reclaiming the Young Offender 1914-48* Oxford: Clarendon Press

Baldwin (1991) *Young People in 1991,* cited in Ashton, 1993

Belson, W. (1975) *Juvenile Theft: The Causal Factors* London: Harper and Row

Blumstein, A. and Cohen, J. (1979) Estimation of individual crime rates from arrest records. *Journal of Criminal Law and Criminology* 70, 561-585

Blumstein, A., Farrington, D. and Moitra, S. (1985) Delinquency careers: innocents, desisters and persisters. In Tonry, M. and Morris, N. (eds) *Crime and Justice* vol.6 Chicago: University of Chicago Press

Bottoms, A.E. (1974) On the decriminalisation of English juvenile courts. In Hood, R. (ed) *Crime, Criminology and Public Policy* London: Heinemann

Campbell, B. (1993) *Goliath: Britain's Dangerous Places* London: Methuen

Cavadino, M. and Dignan, J (1992) *The Penal System: An Introduction* London:Sage

Clarke, J. (1980) Social democratic delinquents and fabian familes. In National Deviancy Conference (ed) *Permissiveness and Control: The Fate of Sixties Legislation* London: Macmillan

Department of Health and Social Security (1981) *Offending by Young People: A Survey of Recent Trends* London: HMSO

Ditchfield, J. (1976) *Police Cautioning in England and Wales* Home Office Research Study No.37 London: HMSO

Dunlop, A. and McCabe, S. (1965) *Young Men in Detention Centres* London: Routledge and Kegan Paul

Evans, R. and Wilkinson, C. (1990) Variations in police cautioning policy and practice in England and Wales. *Howard Journal of Criminal Justice* 29

Farrington, D. (1979) Longitudinal research on crime and delinquency. In Tonry, M. and Morris, N. (eds) *Crime and Justice* Vol.1 Chicago: University of Chicago Press

Farrington, D. (1983) *Further Analysis of a Longitudinal Survey of Crime and Delinquency* Washington DC: National Institute for Justice

Farrington, D. (1984) England and Wales. In Klein, M. (ed) *Western Systems of Juvenile Justice* Beverly Hills: Sage

Farrington, D. (1986) Age and Crime. In Tonry, M. and Morris, N. (eds) *Crime and Justice* Vol.7 Chicago: University of Chicago Press

Farrington, D. (1990) Age, period, cohort and offending, in D.M. Gottfriedson and R.V. Clarke (eds) *Policy and Theory in Criminal Justice: Contributions in Honour of Leslie T. Wilkins* Aldershot: Avebury

Farrington, D. and Bennett, T. (1981) Police cautioning of juveniles in London. *British Journal of Criminology* 21: 123-35

Farrington, D. and West, D. (1990) The Cambridge Study in Delinquent Development: A long-term follow-up of 411 London males. In Kerner, H. and Kaiser, G. (eds) *Criminality: Personality, Behaviour, Life History*, Heidelberg, Germany: Springer-Verlag

Farrington, D. and West, D. (1993) Criminal, Penal and Life Histories of Chronic Offenders: Risk and protective factors and early identification. *Criminal Behaviour and Mental Health,* 3, pp492-523

Faulkner, D.E.R. (1992) Magistrates in the Youth Court. *The Magistrate* September

Gallup/Wrangler (1992) *The Youth Report,* cited in Ashton, 1993

Garland, D. (1985) *Punishment and Welfare: A History of Penal Strategies* Aldershot: Gower

Gottfredson, M.R. and Hirschi, T. (1990) *A General Theory of Crime* Stanford: Stanford University Press

Graham, J. and Moxon, D. (1986) Some trends in juvenile justice *Home Office Research Bulletin* 22: 10-13

Graef, R. (1993) *Living Dangerously* London: Harper Collins

Gurr, T.R. (1976) *Rogues, Rebels and Reformers* London: Sage

Harris, R. and Webb, D. (1987) *Welfare, Power and Juvenile Justice* London: Tavistock

Harwin, J. (1982) The battle for the delinquent. In Jones, C. and Stevenson, J. (eds) *The Yearbook of Social Policy in Britain, 1980-81* London: Routledge and Kegan Paul

Hirschi, T. and Gottfredson, M.R. (1983) Age and the explanation of crime. *American Journal of Sociology,* 89

Home Affairs Committee (1993) *Juvenile Offenders* Sixth Report London: HMSO

Home Office and others (1976) *Children and Young Persons Act 1969: Observations on the Eleventh Report of the Expenditure Committee* Cmnd 6494 London: HMSO

Home Office (1979) *Committee of Inquiry into the United Kingdom Prison Services* Cmnd 7673 London: HMSO

Home Office (1984) *Tougher Regimes in Detention Centres: Report of an Evaluation by the Young Offender Psychology Unit* London: HMSO

Home Office (1988) *Punishment, Custody and the Community* Cm 424 London: HMSO

Home Office Statistical Department (1985) *Criminal Careers of those born in 1953, 1958, 1963.* Statistical Bulletin No.5/89 London: Home Office Statistical Department

Hough, M. and Mayhew, P. (1985) *Taking Account of Crime: Key Findings from the 1984 British Crime Survey* Home Office Research Study No.85 London: HMSO

Hudson, F. and Ineichen, B. (1991) *Taking it Lying Down: Sexuality and Teenage Motherhood* Basingstoke: Macmillan

Knight, B. and West, D. (1975) Temporary and continuing delinquency. *British Journal of Criminology* 15, 43-50

Laycock, G. and Tarling, R. (1985) Police force cautioning policy and practice in England and Wales. *Howard Journal of Criminal Justice*, 24

Mair, G. (1991) *Part-Time Punishment: The Origins and Development of Senior Attendance Centres* London: HMSO

May, M. (1973) Innocence and experience: the evolution of the concept of juvenile delinquency in the mid-nineteenth century. *Victorian Studies* 17,(1)

Mayhew, P., Elliott, D. and Dowds, L. (1989) *The 1988 British Crime Survey* Home Office Research Study No.111 London: HMSO

Measham, F, Newcombe R & Parker H (1993). The post-heroin generation. *Druglink* May/June 1993, pp16-17

Morris, A. and Giller, H. (1987) *Understanding Juvenile Justice* Beckenham: Croom Helm

Muncie, J. (1984) *The Trouble With Kids Today* London: Hutchinson

NACRO (1987) *Diverting Juveniles from Custody: Findings from the Fourth Census of the Projects Funded under the DHSS Intermediate Treatment Initiative.* London: NACRO Juvenile Crime Section

NACRO (1989) *Progress Through Partnership* London: NACRO

NACRO (1993) *Evidence to the Home Affairs Committee* London: NACRO

NCH (1993) *Setting the Record Straight: Juvenile Crime in Perspective* London: NCH

Osborn, S.G. and West, D. (1979) Conviction records of fathers and sons compared. *British Journal of Criminology* 19, 120-133

Osborn, S.G. and West, D. (1980) Do young delinquents really reform? *Journal of Adolescence* 3, 99-114

Ouston, J. (1984) Delinquency, family background and educational attainment. *British Journal of Criminology* 24, 2-26

Pearson, G. (1975) *The Deviant Imaginations* London: Macmillan

Pearson, G. (1983) *Hooligan: A History of Respectable Fears*. London: Macmillan.

Platt, A. (1969) *The Child Savers* Chicago: University of Chicago Press

Platt, A. (1978) *The Child Savers* Chicago: Universityof Chicago Press

Radzinowicz, L. and King, J. (1977) *The Growth of Crime* London: Hamish Hamilton

Reiss, A. and Farrington, D. (1991) Advancing knowledge about co-offending: results from a prospective longitudinal survey of London males. *Journal of Criminal Law and Criminology* 82, 360-95

Riley, D. and Shaw, M. (1985) *Parental Supervision and Juvenile Delinquency* Home Office Research Study No.83 London: HMSO

Rutherford, A. (1986) *Growing Out of Crime: Society and Young People in Trouble* Harmondsworth: Penguin

Rutter, M. and Giller, H. (1983) *Juvenile Delinquency: Trends and Perspectives* Harmondsworth: Penguin

Smith, D.J. (1994 forthcoming) Youth Crime and conduct disorders.: Sociocultural patterns and time trends. In, Rutter, M. and Smith, D.J. (eds) *Psychosocial Problems of Youth in Europe* London: Wiley

Stevenson, S. (1989) Some social and political tides affecting the development of juvenile justice 1938-64. In Gorst, A., Johnman, L. and Lucas, W.S. (eds) *Post-War Britain: Themes and Perspectives, 1945-64* London: Pinter Press and the Institute of Contemporary British History

Tarling, R. (1993) *Analysing Offending: Data, Models and Interpretations* London: HMSO

Taylor, I., Walton, P. and Young, J. (1973) *The New Criminology: For a Social Theory of Deviance* London: RKP

Thane, P. (1981) Childhood in History, in M. King (ed) *Childhood, Welfare and Justice* London: Bedford

Thorpe, D.H, Smith, D., Green, C.J. and Paley, J.G. (1980) *Out of care: the Community Support of Juvenile Offenders* London: George Allen and Unwin

Tutt, N. and Giller, H. (1983) Manifesto for management – the elimination of custody. *Justice of the Peace* 151, 200-2

Wadsworth, M.E.J. (1979) *Roots of Delinquency* London: Martin Robertson

West, D. (1982) *Delinquency: Its Roots, Careers and Prospects* London: Heinemann Educational

West, D. and Farrington, D. (1977) *The Delinquent Way of Life* London: Heinemann Educational

Willis, P. (1977) *Learning to Labour* Aldershot: Gower

Windlesham, Lord (1993) *Responses to Crime (vol 2): Penal Policy in the Making* Oxford: Oxford University Press

Wolfgang, M., Figlio, R.M., and Sellin, T. (1972) *Delinquency in a Birth Cohort.* Chicago: University of Chicago Press

Appendices

A1 Recording form for collecting police information

ID [ ]

PART ONE - For interviewing purposes
Please write in BLOCK CAPITALS.

PERSONAL DETAILS

(1) Name ....

(2) Aliases ....
....

(3) Sex   M/F ....

(4) Date of Birth

[ ][ ][ ][ ] [ ][ ] [ ][ ] [ ]
Day   Month   Year

xx   xx   xx   xx

(5) Ethnicity?

[ ] [ ]
xx   xx

(6) Any sexual offences on the CR? Y/N.

(7) Comments? ....
....

ADDRESSES

(8) Last known address ....
....
....
....

(9) Other possibilities ....
....
....
....

(10) Parent or guardian's name & address if
different. ....
....
....

LATER COMMENTS
Parental permission? Y/N. Date? ....Comments?........

Interviewed? Y/N. Date? .... By? .... Where? ....

Complete/partial information? .... Comments? ....

P A R T   T W O - Arrests in 1992 (see coding notes for details)

ID ☐

(1) TOTAL number of OFFENCES in 1992? ☐

(2) Details of each:

NO.	OFFENCE DATE	ARREST DATE	CLASSIFICATION/DESCRIPTION	£	BAIL Off.	Co.	ACTION	RESULT	COURT DATE

A2   List of questions in the interview schedule

Background
First of all, what is your date of birth?
Are you still at school? If no, what are you doing now?
Who do you live with here?
So is this your parents'/grandparents/foster parents' home? Or is it a
community/children's home?
How long have you lived here?
IF LESS THAN A MONTH: Where did you live before?
IF ANSWERS DON'T COVER 1992: Where were you living for the longest time last
year, in 1992? How long did you live there?
How would you describe your race or ethnic origin?
Do you have any children of your own?
Household social class
Does your mother have a job?
What is the full title of her job?
What position/grade/rank does she have?
Did she have to have any qualifications for this job?
Does she have any other people working under her?
Does your father have a job?
What is the full title of his job?
What position/grade/rank does he have?
Did he have to have any qualifications for this job?
Does he have any other people working under him?
Relationships with parents
Do you have a mother or someone that you consider to be your mother?
And who is that?
How well or badly do you get on with your mother (grandmother, foster mother etc)?
Has your relationship with her changed at all in the last year - have you grown closer or
less close?
Do you have a father or someone that you consider to be your father?
And who is that?
How well or badly do you get on with your father (grandfather, foster father etc)?
Has your relationship with him changed at all in the last year - have you grown closer or
less close?
Have you ever run away from home (or the place where you were living) for one or more
nights without their permission & without telling them where you were going?
How old were you when you did this first?
How many times did you run away from home (or the place that you were living) last
year in 1992?
Social services contact
Have you ever had a supervision order put on you by the court?
Have you ever been in care?
IF YES: Was this in a foster home or in a children's home? Or somewhere else?
Overall, how do you get on with people who worked in the childrens' home(s)?

While you were in residential care, did you ever run away overnight?

How did you get on with the other people in the home? Did you make friends there?

IF NO CONTACT MENTIONED YET: Have you ever had any contact with social services?

IF CONTACT MENTIONED: Have you ever had any other contact with social workers? Overall, how do you get on with social workers? I mean, people like your social worker.

Educational experiences

Just to recap, you said that you were/were not at school at the moment, is that right?

Which secondary school(s) do you/did you go to? IF MORE THAN ONE: Which one did you go to for the longest?

Would you say the standard of your school work is/was above average for your year?

Would you say that you had trouble with your reading at school? Did you see m to be behind most other people in the class?

IF YES: Did you ever get any extra help with your reading at school? Did you have any extra lessons, for example, or go into special classes?

How far would you like to go with your education?

Have you (did you) ever taken time off school when you should have been there? That doesn't include time for illness or anything like that, I just mean skipping school.

How old were you when you played truant for the first time?

Did the school ever do anything about you deliberately missing time?

Thinking back to last year, did you skip any school when you would have been there? How much time do you think you missed last year?

Last year, did you ever do anything that would have got you into trouble with the police (like shoplifting or driving cars or anything like that) while you were truanting from school? I only need you to say yes or no, I don't need to know what it was.

Do you/did you get into fights with other people at school?

Do you/did you get into serious trouble with the teachers? Eg, sent out of classes, kept behind, fight with them?

Do you/did you get bullied there?

Were you ever suspended or expelled or excluded?

What for?

What happened as a result of your explusion (or exclusion?)

Friends

Where did you meet most of your friends?

Are your closest friends about the same age as you, or do they tend to be older or younger than you?

Apart from school, about how many times a week do you see your friends (outside home)?

Is that usually, just one person/two or three/a bigger group?

Boys or girls or both?

Do your parents (or the people you live with) disapprove of any of them?

Do your friends ever disapprove of some of the things you do?

What do they disapprove of?

Do you ever get into trouble with the police when you're with your friends?

Do you ever get into fights with other people? In the street, or in pubs or at football matches, things like that?

Is this with your friends, or when you're on your own?

Do your friends usually have more money, less money, or about the same as you to spend on things like food & going out each week?

How much money do you spend a week on average?

Are your friends now the same as the ones you had last year?

Offending

COMPLETION OF SELF-REPORT OFFENDING LIST.

Have you ever been arrested?

How old were you when you were first arrested?

What for?

What happened?

Generally, if you think about things like shop-lifting, how serious would you say it is to steal something worth £15 from a shop?

If you stole something worth about £15 from a shop TOMORROW, how likely is it that you would be caught by the police for it?

And if they did catch you TOMORROW, and you were arrested, how likely is it that you would ever have to go to court for it?

Thinking next about stealing cars and driving them away (TWOC, TDA), how serious would you say it is to do that?

And if you did steal a car TOMORROW, how likely is it that you would be caught by the police for it?

And if they did catch you TOMORROW, and you were arrested, how likely is it that you would ever have to go to court for it?

Suppose you were on bail after being arrested, so that you had a date to go back to the police or to go to court. How serious would it be to commit another offence while you were on bail? (eg, shoplifting or stealing a car)

And how likely is it that you'd be caught for doing that?

If you were arrested for something like stealing cars or shoplifting, say tomorrow, how long would it be before the courts sentenced you for it?

Have you ever been kept in custody by the courts, either by the local authority or in a YOI?

Some people your age get into quite a bit of trouble with the police. Some never do. Why do some kids your age get involved in crime?

And is that the main reason why you got into trouble, do you think?

Some people carry on getting into trouble, others stop. What do you think stops people?

Is there anything or anyone that you think might help you to keep out of trouble?

Overall, has anyone positive ever come out of your contact with the police and the courts?

Health, drugs, alcohol

Have you had any major illnesses over the last year? Something that has kept you at home or in hospital for a fortnight or more?

What was that?

Do you have any other types of physical difficulties that affect your life? Like asthma, epilepsy, those kinds of things?

Have you ever drunk alcohol?

In an average week, how many days do you drink alcohol?

On an average day when you drink, how much do you have?

Have you ever been really drunk?

How often do you get really drunk in an average month?

Have you ever had problems with your family because of drinking? Like someone arguing with you about it, or throwing you out or something like that?

Have you had problems with your friends because of your drinking? Like people arguing with you about it, or causing trouble over it?

Have you ever taken cannabis (marijuana, grass, hash, ganja, blow, spliff, joint...)

Have you ever tried any drugs apart from cannabis, or sniffed glue or anything like that?

SELF-COMPLETE DRUG LIST

Have you ever had problems with your family because of taking drugs? Like someone arguing with you about it, or throwing you out or something like that?

Have you had problems with your friends because of taking drugs? Like people arguing with you about it, or causing trouble over it?

Psychological services

Have you ever seen a psychologist or a psychiatrist?

Or has anyone ever arranged for you to talk to someone about problems that you might have had?

What for?

Who arranged that?

The future

To sum up, generally, how do you feel about the way things are going? How satisfied are you with your life at the moment?

What do you think you will be doing this time next year?

And how about in five years time?

Interviewer ratings

Duration of interview

Where interviewed

Quality of information

Others present, who.

Cooperation of interviewee

Tone of interview

Gender of interviewee

A3   Self-report offences list

List of things you might have done

FOR EACH ITEM:
PLEASE CIRCLE '0' IF YOU HAVE NEVER DONE IT,
OR CIRCLE '1' IF YOU HAVE.

	NO	YES	How of IN LAS MONTH
Travelled on a bus, train or tube without paying your fare	0	1	_____
Driven a car without a licence and/or insurance	0	1	_____
Driven a care without a licence, or were disqualified	0	1	_____
Driven a car or moped when you've drunk more than the limit	0	1	_____
Damaged something, like a phone box, house windows etc	0	1	_____
Written graffiti	0	1	_____
Got into an 18 certificate film by lying about your age	0	1	_____
Stolen money from a gas or electricity meter, public phone, vending machine, video game machine etc	0	1	_____
Stolen anything from any kind of shop	0	1	_____
Stolen anything from someone's home	0	1	_____
Stolen anything from a car	0	1	_____
Taken a car, motorbike or moped without the owner's permission (TWOC, TDA)	0	1	_____
Stolen something from a person, like a purse or bag	0	1	_____
Sneaked into a house or building intending to steal something	0	1	_____
Bought or sold something you knew was stolen	0	1	_____
Sold a cheque book, credit card, cash point card, belonging to someone else	0	1	_____
Carried a weapon (knife, gun) to use to defend yourself	0	1	_____
Threatened someone with a weapon to try to get them to give you something	0	1	_____
Got into a fight in public somewhere, at the football, outside the pub, etc	0	1	_____
Bought drugs for your own use	0	1	_____
Sold drugs to someone else	0	1	_____
Set fire to something on purpose	0	1	_____
Hurt someone (not in your family) enough to cause some injury	0	1	_____

A4   Description of offence type

Offence type	Includes
Burglary (res)	Burglary, dwelling/residential
Burglary (other)	Burglary, Burglary & Theft (business, other) Burglary, B & T UNSPECIFIED Burglary with intent Attempted burglary (of any kind) Aid & abet any of these
Aggravated car theft	Aggravated Theft of m/v, Agg TWOC, Agg TDA Aggravated CARRY (ditto)
Car theft	Theft of m/v, car, moped, van, TWOC, TDA Allowing to be carried, Carry TWOC, Carry TDA Attempted theft of m/v, attempted TWOC etc
Theft from car	Theft from m/v Vehicle interference, Interference, MV Int
Theft from person	Theft from person Attempted theft from person
Theft from shop	Theft from shops (shoplifting, Theft S/L) Attempted theft from shops
Theft of pedal cycle	Attempted theft of cycle
Theft unspecified	Theft UNSPECIFIED Attempted theft UNSPECIFIED
Going equipped	Going equipped to steal
Stolen goods	Handling stolen goods, HSG, Handling Receiving stolen goods, RSG, Receiving Making off without payment Obtaining by by deception Fraud or forgery Attempted, any of these
Robbery	Robbery Attempted robbery, Robbery with intent

ABH	Actual bodily harm Common assault, assault, ABH Attempted ABH, attempted assault ABH with intent
GBH	Grievious bodily harm Malicious wounding Attempted GBH GBH with intent
Criminal Damage +	(Crim dam, Damage, CD) Attempted CD, CD with intent Arson
Drugs offences	Possession of a class B drug (cannabis) Possession of a class A drug Other drug offences
Traffic offences	
	Reckless driving, Without due care & attention Drunk driving Disqualified driving (driving without licence, underage driving) No licence No insurance No tax, mot, no test certificate, etc Other road traffic offences (RTA, running red lights, failure to stop etc) Aid & abet any of these
Bail & procedural offences	
	Breach of Bail (Bail Act Offence, Breach, failure to surrender to bail) Breach of CD Failure to appear at court Contempt of court
Sexual offences	Prostitution (soliciting, loitering) Unlawful sexual intercourse (USI, underage sex, sex with minor) Indecent assault Indecent exposure Buggery

Rape

Public order

Threatening behaviour, threat to damage,
Disorderly conduct,
Public order offence, POA offence,
 application to bind over
Violent Disorder (POA S.2)
Affray (POA S.3)
Possession of an offensive weapon
Drunkenness offences (drunk & disorderly)

Other

Cruelty to animals
Being in an enclosed area
Misc

A5   Table 8.3   Contact with social services

	Full Sample	Definition one group	Definition two group	Definition three group
Proportion 'known' to s. services	51%	97%	90%	84%
First contact - supervision order	9%	31%	31%	33%
First contact - accomm'd compulsorily	9%	21%	14%	2%